DRAMA AND THE THEATRE

with Radio, Film and Television

An outline for the student

Contributors

J. F. Arnott
Clive Barker
George Brandt
John Russell Brown
John Fernald
Kenneth Muir
Kenneth Parrott
Gordon Vallins
Graham Woodruff

Edited by John Russell Brown

*Head of the Department of Drama
and Theatre Arts University of Birmingham*

DRAMA AND THE THEATRE

with Radio, Film and Television

An outline for the student

Routledge & Kegan Paul   London

First published 1971
by Routledge & Kegan Paul Ltd
Broadway House,
68–74 Carter Lane,
London, EC4V 5EL

Printed in Great Britain by
C. Tinling & Co. Ltd, Prescot and London

ISBN 0 7100 6971 5 (C)
ISBN 0 7100 7053 5 (P)

Contents

Illustrations

Introduction

The Study of Drama and Theatre

John Russell Brown

When Hamlet says 'To be or not to be' on the stage of a subsidized national theatre, a hundred and more persons will have contributed at first hand towards making that moment exactly what it is. Governors of the theatre, administrators, director and designer, fellow actors, scene painters and costume makers, stage manager, production manager, lighting consultant and all their assistants – all members of the company and organization – will have collaborated in a process that has led to this particular dramatic moment. The front-of-house staff, the critics, scholars and advertisement experts, everyone who has helped to draw the particular audience of that night and everyone who has made the actor and the audience what they are will influence the effect of those words. The repercussions of the dramatic event are moral and political, intellectual, emotional and instinctive, traditional, social and individual. In short, a theatrical moment is infinitely complicated, and anyone wishing to study plays in performance has ahead of him a huge and endless task.

Yet when someone says he is interested in a career in the theatre, the odds are that the first response will be: 'Do you want to be an actor?' or, rather, 'You don't want to be an actor, do you?' This challenge is made so readily because the theatre can seem very simple, a matter of personal and direct response to the art of the actor. Everyone play-acts in life, and can thus feel at home in the stage's reality or else can imagine that others feel this need to identify intensely and completely.

1

Many enthusiasts of the theatre do indeed attempt a career in acting, but few succeed. Equity, the union of the profession in Great Britain, is actively considering the problems of over-crowding and the plight of many trained actors who cannot follow their chosen career. Unemployment is high and average yearly earnings dangerously low. While it is clear that large numbers of people have a talent for acting – almost everyone can pretend and imitate, and many are capable of the imagina-tive creation of a person different from themselves – the ability to sustain a career as an actor, performing nightly on a stage in such a way as to draw large audiences, seems to be a very rare endowment. Moreover, the theatre in Great Britain today offers very few opportunities for the proper development of such an ability even when it does unmistakably manifest itself.

An interest in theatre may well start with the desire to act, but this is by no means a true indication of where that interest should lead. A response to theatre implies an active imagina-tion, a mind and being stimulated by other people, by words, colours, shapes, movements, rhythms and melody, by culture, social relationships and oneself, by an instinct for the essential. To study theatre is to be involved in discovery about oneself and others, and to gain a growing knowledge of the world in which we live.

As the study of theatre should know few bounds, so the careers to which this preparation may lead are numerous, within the theatre itself and outside it. Besides actors, the production of plays calls for directors, administrators, stage staff, designers, musicians, playwrights, historians, critics, voice experts, choreographers and so on. In education, teachers are needed for dramatic literature, for creative drama, theatre history and theatre skills. Posts in television, films, advertising, personnel management, public relations, arts administration, community centre and youth club work can all make direct use of talents developed and knowledge gained from a study of drama and theatre.

For the intending student there are, clearly, two main problems: where to begin and how to find direction for individual talent. But for professional teachers many other questions remain. What is the best introduction to each branch of study? How wide should be the syllabus, and where its centre? What basic knowledge is required? What academic organization and sequence of study will be most helpful? How can individual students collaborate with each other in group practical work? What form of discipline is needed, what challenges, what opportunities and freedom? Most institutions offering courses in drama and theatre are not much older than this century – in Great Britain, all university departments of drama were founded after the second world war – and for educational bodies this is tenderest youth, when boldness, uncertainty and diversity are still everywhere apparent.

This is, indeed, a fine time for learning, for both teacher and student, with new techniques of research and new concepts of theatre and of education banishing routine and laziness. It is a time of active discovery and a growing realization of the theatre's opportunities as an educative medium. There are frustrations due to limited physical facilities and shortage of staff and money for what is, comparatively, an expensive subject to teach. But these can be borne or by-passed when there is already so much to do, and when the spirit of adventure thrives and responsibility is nourished.

The true danger for student and teacher in this exploratory phase is confusion of purposes, usually accompanied by a lack of intellectual rigour on the one hand and, on the other, by an artistic complacency. Intentions should be stated and the work limited in consequence; greediness and fear of criticism have to be guarded against.

An intending student will usually start by seeing a simple way ahead: he wants to act, or design, or write or teach. But he may well be mistaken in his abilities, especially if he sees himself as an actor. At the beginning it is well to remember the potential scope of theatre studies and realize that there are many ways from which the student can choose. To give an impression of this great scope it may be helpful to try to imagine the 'complete student', one who is capable of respond-ing in all possible ways.

First he would want to understand such theatrical experiences as he has already encountered. He will want to know how a theatre operates, what is a good play or a good production, why one actor dominates all others in performance. He will be curious about forms of theatre that he has not yet met, and so will turn to theatre history, read plays of other times and places, and trace the careers and respond to the manifestoes of famous theatre workers of his own and other ages.

All this verbal description, theory, history and criticism will be hard to study without some attendance at productions, and the more the better. But just as it is hard to judge the talents of a swimmer or a pianist if one has not swum or played an instrument, so a first-hand acquaintance with the processes of rehearsal and production will enormously increase the student's ability to visualize the dramatic events that lie behind the testimony of play-texts, histories, memoirs or theatre ground-plans. Such practical studies are common in other academic subjects, so that few students would choose to study, say, German language and literature without trying to speak German. We are sometimes asked to study a 'dead' language, but the oral practice of a language is obviously a great help to the student's capacity to appreciate its structure, rhythms, nuances and force. And so it is with drama, except that the 'language' of the theatre is very much more complicated, for it includes space, movement and form as well as sound, time and words, and relies upon the individual skills and beings of numerous and ever-changing human agents. When a student is first introduced to the practical conditions of performance as part of his study of drama, he will often cease to be a theoretician or critic on the spot: so many new facets and new problems of definition are at once revealed. But the practical and historical, the critical and theoretical theatre studies may go hand-in-hand; it is usually best for them to alternate as need and opportunity dictate.

The practical work of the 'complete student' will be of two kinds: first, the exploratory and demonstratory support for his attempt to understand what happens in performance; and, secondly, the means of learning how to create drama himself. The two kinds are best kept separate, for the speed of academic study is quite different from that of creative development; and their standards and demands are different.

In developmental work the student will at once confront his personal limitations. These are of little concern to his pursuit of theatrical knowledge in general (although the more skilled

he is as actor, designer or director, the further can his knowledge and appreciation extend), but they are crucial to the
young artist. Drama explores extremes of human conduct and
feeling, and so the student will constantly confront situations
in his work which are beyond the range of his experience to
handle and his ability to express. To engage in these situations
demands, therefore, that the student shed inhibitions and
repressions, and discard such defensive mechanisms by which
we all ordinarily protect ourselves from painful experiences.
He must seek to know himself, and this will inevitably reveal
the present limitations of his personal resources and practical
abilities; and it may well involve physical and emotional crises
along the way. The young actor must also be patient, content
to work within a very small range before tackling the larger
problems, for there is little to be learnt from continually failing
to reach one's objectives. Yet failure is also vital, for this is the
point at which development is seen to be necessary; and so,
from the beginning, risks should be taken, with a teacher's
guidance and also, probably, without any help at all.

The practical studies of the young artist will call upon his
honesty, imagination, strength, patience and courage, and in
all this he is essentially alone. Yet, on another level, his studies
will be co-operative and immediately rewarding. He will find
many aids. First, anatomy and medical science, to understand
and take care of the physical instrument that is himself as an
actor. Then, the study of music, dance, movement and voice
provides some basis for discipline and for objective knowledge.
Exercises in observation, invention and improvisation are
available for the actor, although many of these need experienced leaders if they are not to encourage self-absorbed or
possibly dangerous activity. An introductory course in design
that teaches an understanding of colour, form, light and line
will extend knowledge and creative ability beyond the narrow
focus of an individual actor or group of figures. For the student
of stage design, this is the beginning of many studies, which will
include architecture, acoustics, painting, modelling, construction, lighting.

The work will seem endless, but so it should. Art is demanding when it seeks a controlled expression of a response to life,
and drama is peculiar in finding its expression through the

agency of living human beings and their context. Drama makes unparalleled demands for self-knowledge and self-control in those who try to practise it.

With his curiosity challenged and his creativity given scope to work, the 'complete student' will wish to explore various extensions of his theatrical experience. He will want to understand film, television, opera, ballet. He will study ways in which theatre can satisfy audiences and will learn about its political, religious, educational and therapeutic uses. He will ask whether it functions as fulfilment of desires and fantasies, or as escape from life, or as continual exploration and quest, or as a means of clarifying, judging and heightening social existence. He will try to relate a theatre to the society that supports it and is, perhaps, supported by that theatre.

Finally, and all the time and in all his studies, the student will be educating himself. He will have learnt something about the society in which he lives, its history, structure and means of communication. He will have studied play-texts and other evidence of theatrical productions from all the great ages of civilization. He will be more acutely aware of the expressiveness of language and movement, and will have observed himself alone and in relationship to others, in imaginary and varied situations and states of being. He will be able to 'read' a complicated encounter or confrontation in real life, as on a stage. He will have begun to respond to the many different arts that contribute to theatre, the 'fine arts' and many directly useful arts. He will have been encouraged to ask the reason and effectiveness of everything.

In view of the scope of the study of drama and theatre, it is no wonder that many different and variedly specialized courses are offered. Each country has its own pattern in this, depending on the schools programme and the financial, artistic and academic basis of its professional theatre. One of the peculiarities of drama education in Britain is the foundation of acting schools independent of any particular theatre; in other European countries, many of the larger theatres train their own recruits. At the other extreme, our vocational drama schools usually lack the context of a university which is common in the United States and not infrequent elsewhere in Europe, especially in the East. Great Britain is among the most advanced countries, however, in training for educational theatre, in both teacher training colleges and in subsidiary courses in vocational schools and universities.

In common with other countries, the situation here is developing and changing from year to year. The Appendix to this book, on Courses for Students of Drama and Theatre, gives sources of information rather than precise details, for all the time new courses are being developed and old ones allowed to lapse. Some interesting statistics were collected on the occasion of the first American College Theatre Festival in Washington, D.C., in 1969. Since 1962, the number of teachers and students specializing in Drama in the United States had trebled. 1,600 American colleges offered regular theatre instruction: there were over 4,000 teachers; and over 100,000 students took part in theatrical productions – still more took courses in theatre.

In considering British practice, attention should be given first to the oldest, and by far the most numerous, of the courses offered, those in plays and dramatists, notably in Shakespeare and the English tradition. Many institutions of 'Higher Education' offer these subjects; in fact, few do not. But the majority of the courses are isolated from the study of other aspects of theatre and find their place in the syllabus for English Literature, General Studies or other literatures, such as French, German, Italian and so forth. Students examine play-texts and are especially concerned with style, structure, theme, and the play's reflection of the life and ideas of the author's time and country. Unfortunately, these studies are not always related to an understanding of the conditions of performance, without which a play's theatrical life cannot be fully realized. Yet sometimes there are classes in theatre practice or theatre history in support of more literary studies. Almost always there are groups of students, with or without official recognition, who try to stage one or two of the plays studied in each academic year. Such practical support for the study of play-texts is developing year by year, but it is often little more than uninformed skirmishing with an essential difficulty in the study of all that is called 'dramatic literature', whether long-established and much debated like Shakespeare, or the uncertain first scripts of new writers. A student whose interest in literature is primarily centred on dramatic texts would be most satisfied working within a drama department's course or in definite and continual relationship to one.

For students who want to learn to act or to design for the theatre, or to stage-manage, and whose interest is quite clearly dependent on the practice of these arts without much concern for the larger issues of theatre, the best courses are those at drama schools and colleges of art. There are two- and three-year courses and, for design, up to four-year courses. Some courses involve productions or design projects with professionally active guest teachers. At drama schools, the last two terms are usually spent preparing a group of productions that can be seen by prospective employers and actors' agents. Several of the larger schools now have television and film facilities as well as studios and stages, so that the student actor may, from his earliest days, be versatile and at home in the newer media. Most schools have an eclectic attitude to acting or design styles, but a few believe that, in the interest of strong development, a clear basis and single direction should be provided. An intelligent student will want to scrutinize up-to-date syllabuses for himself and choose accordingly.

In study and training for actors, an early start and a disciplined programme are great advantages. The body and voice acquire bad habits that are more difficult to eradicate the longer they are left untutored, and good coordination, strength and physical resilience need to be inculcated early. Moreover, the actor's creativity and control need to be fostered by continuous opportunity and stimulus. For all these reasons, entrance to a drama school or college of art immediately after secondary school is recommended.

University courses are to be preferred by a student whose desire to create drama goes along with a mind which is curious about all aspects of theatre work, or by one whose curiosity is still his strongest interest in the theatre. For would-be managers, administrators, critics and scholars a university is clearly the best choice. It is probably so for a would-be director also, since he needs knowledge and experience over a very wide range of theatre activity. The courses offered vary greatly, and at some universities it is possible to combine the study of drama with the study of literature and language, or of music, sociology, fine art, history, psychology and so forth. But obviously, a three-year course has its limits, and the danger is that students may attempt too much to master anything thoroughly. The width of studies offered at a university is a danger as well as an attraction. Specialization is needed progressively throughout the course, and if it is possible to choose after testing a wide range of areas, all should be well.

The nature and the quantity of practical work is the clearest difference between drama departments in British universities. Most have adequate to generous physical facilities, but some use these chiefly for productions in which students explore plays and theatrical realities with whatever competence they can muster from their talents and a few preparatory classes. Other drama departments use their studios chiefly for developmental classes and exercises in acting or theatre presentation, and mount full-scale productions only when they will be a support to this basic approach. The difference can be expressed in other terms, by saying that some university teachers believe that practical work supports critical and historical (or 'academic') study, some that acting and other aspects of theatre can be studied only in practical ways and that to be 'academic' means to be patient and to be as questioning about acting as about history, language or any of the other more established university subjects.

There is no simple answer to the question 'What vocational training will be needed after a university course?' At some universities, for some students, 'None' may be an appropriate reply; but this is never a matter of course. No university is a vocational school alone, so that the responsibility for specific training is largely upon the student himself. After three years, for some students, 'You are ready to begin your artistic or specialized training' may be the right answer. All three of the main factors are variable: the individual student; the exact course he has followed; the form of work in the theatre or elsewhere that he wishes to undertake.

The intending student who wishes to teach has several courses open to him. He may go to one of the drama schools that have a Teacher's Diploma course, or to a university that has an optional 'Theatre in Education' specialization or, for the

B

widest educational background, to a teacher's training college offering drama as a major subject. The number of these last is rising steadily, and the range of study is impressive. Among the colleges there is a choice of emphasis upon creative drama, dramatic literature or practical theatre. Many colleges offer a four-year course leading to a Bachelor of Education university degree.

Further opportunities for full-time study are available at technical colleges and colleges of further education. There are two main purposes behind these drama courses: first, to use the subject as a means of general and personal education; and secondly, to provide an introduction to more specialized training at drama schools or elsewhere.

In addition to all these full-time courses, there are evening classes, week-end courses and short residential 'schools' during vacation times, at which the student may sample a wide range of work. The British Drama League; adult colleges; university extramural departments; drama schools; amateur, youth and professional theatres, all offer such opportunities according to local needs. For many people they provide a continuing education in theatre throughout life. If the new and leisured society which some sociologists predict becomes a reality, the importance of these part-time studies may well grow. As a participatory art, drawing on many and various talents and providing entertainment of immediate interest, such a society may well support theatre strongly, and so theatre as we know it today could be transformed; for this to come about study at all levels of involvement will be needed.

The nature of theatre as a subject for study and the ways of studying it are the twin concerns of this present book. All its contributors have practical experience of staging plays for professional or student companies, or for both, and all are active as teachers. Necessarily, attention is chiefly focused on the main elements of plays in performance in theatres, now and in the past. Inevitably there are omissions: theatre architecture, the physique of actors, language, costume, music are not considered in depth; no scene designer, voice consultant or movement teacher is among the contributors. The chosen topics place more specialized studies in a wider context, because such a book as this needs, above all, to give an impression of general scope.

A chapter on Radio, Film and Television is included because so many intending students have more experience of drama in these new media than in theatres, and because much of the present work in theatres themselves is connected with these potentially separate activities. In a longer book, there would have been further chapters on dance and opera, and on puppet theatre.

It would have been possible to compile lists and draw diagrams to express the manifold interests of the subject of drama and theatre. But after this introductory survey, each chapter tries to fill out rather than define and limit, to provide sufficient detail and example to give a taste of the learning experience that is being considered.

1

Theatre History

J. F. Arnott

Most people seem to find something to interest them in the study of the past, even if their interest takes them no further than walking round historic buildings and stops short of actually reading history books. It is difficult to say just why there is this interest in the past, and, no doubt, the full explanation is complex and involves irrational motivation. One thing that could be said, however, is that the past sets standards. An achievement has to be remarkable for good or ill to survive all the destructive processes of time. In history is to be found the inspiration of great men's lives, and warnings of man's capacity for inhumanity to man. In the arts, history provides the achievements against which all later works of art must be measured. One can say, too, that history helps to explain the present. If one cannot know how it will all end, one can at least ask how it all began. I suppose this is the idea behind the journalistic phrase 'the march of history'. Any one individual's experience of time can be only the smallest sample. It is like an instantaneous photograph of a moving action which does not tell us how the action ended, or indeed even the direction of the movement. The study of history, even if it does not fully reveal the secret causes of the rise and fall of civilizations and of art movements, does at least free us from an experience limited to the present. One sometimes meets a prejudice against the study of history as being concerned with the dead past, and of no value to those who are interested in life here and now. History can, however, be a liberating force. It is easy to show how, in

13

politics and in the arts, those who have changed the course of the future have drawn their ideas from the past. The Renaissance means the rebirth of classical culture. The Romantic Movement is also the Mediaeval Revival. One could also cite the influence of oriental drama on Brecht and Artaud. There is, of course, a more limited sense in which the study of the past helps us to understand the present. We have to live our lives in an environment which we have inherited, which contains many features the function of which is no longer clear. We still go to theatres where there is a dress circle in which no one is dressed up; where there are boxes from which one can see the audience better than the stage; and where the stage itself is surrounded by a gilded proscenium like a picture frame, from which, however, the picture has apparently been removed.

The Interpretation of Classics

While it is the definition of a classic that it is not for an age but for all time, revealing meanings to later ages which were not apparent to contemporaries, the passage of time can expose it to misinterpretation. Like the varnish discoloured with age which alters the original colours of an old master, the change in language, in social custom and in theatrical conditions obscures the original quality of a play. The nineteenth-century scholars gave us excellent editions of the mediaeval miracle plays, but because they could not see beyond the realistic dramatic methods of their own time, they dismissed the mediaeval playwrights as unskilful. With the rise of perspective scenery in the seventeenth century, the stage-craft of Shakespeare was misunderstood, and for over two centuries his plays were never presented as he wrote them. If one is to be sure that one understands a classic, one must have regard to its historical context. A knowledge of the history of the theatre is almost essential if one is producing plays of the past. This is not to say that the modern production of a classic need be an archaeological reconstruction, though it is worth noting that some of the most successful of contemporary productions of classics have, in fact, incorporated features taken with little change from the original setting. What is necessary is that the present-day director should have some knowledge of the original principles of staging and of the original actor-audience relationship. He may then revive them or, as he will usually choose to do, find their modern equivalents. The alternative, chosen by some twentieth-century directors, of ignoring the original form and meaning of a classic seems to me to result in productions which are only of interest as experiments. They can never be finished artistic achievements because inevitably they involve clashes of style between the old and the new. In any case, they seem pointless. A classic is a sort of artistic oracle, and we do not consult the oracle to put words into its mouth.

The Methods of Theatre History

For some, history is a pure science; they wish to discover the historical truth as an end in itself. For others, history is an applied science; they wish to make use of their historical knowledge in their particular spheres of action. The statesman and the military commander are examples that will spring to mind, but there are theatrical historians in the second camp, too. One of the greatest historians of the mediaeval theatre, Gustave Cohen, after a long lifetime devoted to writing scholarly works on the subject, regarded as his crowning achievement the founding of a theatre company to present mediaeval plays in the original style.

A practical commitment may be a dangerous quality in a theatrical historian. One can see this danger very clearly in other areas of history. We have considered history as the lives of great men, but political or religious interests may make men into heroes and martyrs. The man who played a part in history is replaced by the figure on the banner or the political poster. We have also used the phrase 'the march of history', but you might get a very different account of the itinerary from the Marxist and the Christian, and even from the Protestant and the Catholic. The same is true of theatre history. A modern writer on the theatre who is also a director attracted by the artistic possibilities of theatre-in-the-round may find the theatre-in-the-round everywhere in mediaeval and Elizabethan drama, which seems to me to be forcing the evidence.

It is clear that the history of the theatre is of no value unless it is genuine history. To discover what in fact happened in the theatre of the past, the student has to employ the traditional methods of scholarship. He must rid his mind of preconceptions. This is difficult to achieve, for it is natural for us to interpret the unfamiliar in terms of the familiar. A scholar accustomed to a theatre in which the curtain rises to reveal a stage already set may be reluctant to accept that scenery could ever have been changed in full view of the audience. Observing the evidence with objectivity, one must follow the argument to whatever conclusion it leads, or, if the evidence is insufficient, be prepared to remain in a state of academic doubt. As to the evidence itself, one must be aware of the distinction between primary and secondary sources, that is, between the original document – for example, the De Witt drawing of the Elizabethan Swan Theatre – and the article or book offering an interpretation of the document. One must learn to go back to the primary source and, ideally, to the original document itself, and not a transcription, though one soon learns the scholars whose transcriptions are to be trusted. The documents will be either printed or manuscript. In the printed category are books, pamphlets, periodicals, playbills, programmes, theatre tickets, large-scale maps – if you look up old directories in your local library you will find that they often contain street plans showing the location of vanished theatres. In the second category are plays in manuscript, prompt books, contracts, documents relating to legal disputes, letters, account books, inventories. Then there is the iconography of the subject, that is, the pictorial records: architects' plans and drawings, designs for scenery and costumes, paintings, engravings, woodcuts and photographs of actors and productions, and, the most recent development, films and telerecordings. There are also sound archives on disc and tape. Occasionally the actual costumes and properties used have been preserved. The student of the history of theatre architecture may have the opportunity to study his material at first hand, although theatres have been less preserved than other types of building. The oldest English theatre, Drury Lane, has undergone vast alterations in its history. The Theatre Royal, Bristol, and the Theatre in Richmond, Yorkshire, still preserve the characteristics of an elegant and of a more modest provincial playhouse of the eighteenth century, and most of our towns and cities still preserve nineteenth-century theatres. Of the Renaissance and Baroque theatres which have survived on the continent, pride of place must be given to Palladio's Teatro Olimpico at Vicenza in Italy. Numerous Greek and Roman theatres have, of course, survived – there is a Roman Theatre at St Albans. Though Shakespeare's Globe has vanished without trace, one can still stand on the site of the theatre of Dionysus in Athens in which the words of the *Agamemnon* of Aeschylus were first spoken some two and a half millennia ago. Some features of the theatre of the time of Aeschylus have been uncovered by archaeological excavation, rather an exceptional technique for the student of theatre history to employ.

While I have given a warning that the theatre history written by practical men of the theatre may be refashioned in the image of their artistic ideals, I should also point out that the findings of those who regard theatre history as a pure and not an applied science may suffer from their lack of practical experience. Here we come to an issue which divides theatre historians into two schools: those who believe that their theories should be wholly based on the examination of documents in accordance with the principles of scholarship; and those who believe that they must also be tested, like the theories of the scientist, by practical experiment. Certainly there are questions which can be answered by an examination of the documents alone – for example, the date of the original production of a play, or the constitution of the audience – but when it is a question of evaluating a stage technique, that is another matter. The art of the theatre is so complex that it is difficult to be sure that a purely theoretical discussion will take account of all the factors involved. A striking result of experiment is the doubt cast on the statement confidently repeated in book after book that the Elizabethan actors first performed in inn-yards: Professor Glynne Wickham discovered, when he was asked to produce a play in a surviving Elizabethan inn-yard, that the practical difficulties were insuperable.

I have spent a good deal of time discussing the techniques of the theatre historian, which may seem surprising in a paper intended to introduce the subject of theatre history. The beginner might have expected instead the names of history books which would give him direct access to the content of the subject. While this might be possible for other branches of history, it is less so for the history of the theatre. There are monumental works of scholarship which cover the general history of the theatre, and there are numerous special studies; but the student will find that there is still a great deal of ground to be covered. He will often find that the questions which interest him most – for example, how a particular part has been played, how a particular play has been directed or what theatres have existed in his locality – have not yet been answered. From an early stage, therefore, he will be involved in research. This, of course, is one of the fascinations of the subject, and many students of theatre history seem quite happy to remain in this detective stage.

Theatre History and Dramatic Literature

Before we go on to discuss the content of the subject, there is a difference of opinion among theatre historians which must be mentioned. One school would include the playwright among the artists of the theatre; the other would leave his contribution to the historian of literature. Two reasons might be suggested for the existence of this second view. It partly arises from what in other circles would be called a demarcation dispute. The university study of dramatic literature is as old as the universities themselves, whereas theatre history has only become a subject in the curriculum during the present century. This is, no doubt, because of the literary bias of the universities and because the materials for the study of literature are much more readily available: the text of the play survives and the records of the acting and staging are lost more often than not. When the new departments of drama and theatre history were established, they had to justify their claims to independent existence by stressing that their field of study was different from that of the established departments of literature and language. In the effort to get clear of the gravitational field of the older departments and achieve independent orbit, the advocates of the new development had to stress what was different in their teaching, but some went too far and denied that there was anything in common with what had gone before. In fact, the demarcation between a department of English and a department of drama does not lie in their studying different materials, but in their different attitude to the same material. As universities which have departments both of language and literature and of drama have recognized, there are good academic grounds for studying a writer like Shakespeare from both the literary and the theatrical point of view. The second reason is of longer standing and is to be found not in universities, but in a perennial dispute within the theatre itself, between the writer on the one hand and the actors, the director or the designer on the other. The earliest historical and critical work on the drama, Aristotle's *Poetics*, a manual of playwriting, speaks slightingly of spectacle. Ben Jonson quarrelled with Inigo Jones, the designer of his court masques. In recent history, we have the differences of opinion between Chekhov and his director Stanislavsky. Gordon Craig writes of the tyranny of the word in the theatre. On a closer examination, however, these disputes will be found not to be confined to poets and actors; they exist equally between actors and designers, between actors and directors, between directors and designers and, most notably, between actresses and actresses. The fact is that the theatre is an art of collaboration and obviously the artists working together will not always see eye to eye. Because the playwright does not always agree with his fellows, however, is no reason for excluding him from our survey, any more than any other artist of the theatre. Moreover, if theatre history affords many examples of the dispute between writers and actors, it provides a vastly greater weight of evidence of their interdependence. In spite of artistic developments like ballet and mime, and experiments by modern *avant-garde* groups with vocalization (that is, the use of the voice to produce sounds, not words), for most of the recorded history of the drama, the literary element has been an integral part of it. Aristotle stresses that action is of first importance in tragedy; but he takes it for granted that human action will be accompanied by speech. It is true that what we follow on the stage is the continuing life of the actor, not a sequence of words; but the actor makes use of words to reveal (or conceal) his thoughts and feelings.

The Starting Point of Theatre History

That the history of drama begins at least as far back as the fifth century B.C., when the Athenian drama was at its height, is evident from the word 'theatre' itself. It is one of the many theatrical terms which come from the Greek, though in some cases the meaning has changed. A Greek *drama*, whether *tragedy* or *comedy*, was witnessed from the *theatre* (or seeing-place) and performed partly by a *chorus* which sang and danced on the *orchestra* (or dancing-place). The songs of the chorus came between the *episodes* performed by the actors on the *proscenium*, the area in front of the *scene*, or stage building. The play opened with a *prologue* and ended with an *epilogue*.

Behind the Athenian drama, unmatched since in many respects, and possessed of this considerable vocabulary of technical terms (and I have recorded only those which are still in use), must lie a long history of development, and, in fact, there are fragmentary records of even older dramatic activity, in Greece and in Egypt. Most remote of all is a Palaeolithic cave painting in the cave of the Trois Frères, near Ariège in France, which shows a dancer disguised as a deer, wearing the animal's skin, a tail, and an antlered head-dress.

Religion and the Drama

In the Trois Frères cave painting, the dancer is clearly acting the part of the deer, and the painting records something dramatic; but from what we know of the oldest societies, we can also say that the dancer was taking part in a magical rite intended in some way to bring success to the tribe in the hunting upon which its survival depended. He exemplifies, therefore, the close relationship of the earliest form of drama with religion. Drama and ritual can be almost indistinguishable as far as form goes: in both, the actor or celebrant engages in imitation by action and word, making use of appropriate costume, objects and settings. It is in the intention and in the kind of belief accorded to the imitator that they differ. The religious celebrant becomes one with his god. The actor merely impersonates the hero. One might say that ritual and drama are the same phenomenon seen from different points of, view, and that ritual passes into drama when the old faith is replaced by a new kind of belief.

The close associations of drama with religion in the beginning are everywhere evident. The Greek drama, according to Aristotle, originated in the rites of Dionysus. Though it had clearly developed from ritual into art, it was still performed at religious festivals. The resolution of many Greek plays is achieved by the appearance of a god, the *deus ex machina*.

The same association can be seen in the drama of China, where shamans assumed the characters of supernatural beings; or in the *nō* plays of Japan. In mediaeval Europe a new dramatic tradition arose within the Christian church. It is still a matter of dispute among scholars if this was a spontaneous development within the church, or was suggested by such professional entertainment as survived, carrying on the tradition of the late classical theatre, in the outside world, or was an attempt to supersede the pagan rituals which survived the advent of Christianity. It is a strange fact of history that magic imitative dances like those of the cave paintings, and other dramatic rituals like the mimic slaying and revival of a leader, though far older than the Greek drama which grew out of them, long survived it, and indeed have survived as folk customs to modern times. These are exemplified by the dance of men wearing antlers at Abbots Bromley, in Staffordshire, and the widespread Mummers' Play in which St George is slain by the Turkish knight and revived by a comic doctor.

Whether mediaeval Christianity generated the first impulse or not, it certainly produced an entirely new dramatic tradition. First came the liturgical plays, so called from their being an extension of the liturgy or church service. The earliest example of a liturgical play is the *Visitatio Sepulchri* (the *Visit to the Tomb*), performed by members of the religious community of Benedictine monasteries in England towards the end of the tenth century. Celebrating the Resurrection and performed at matins on Easter morning before the altar, chanted and sung in the Latin of the church service by members of the religious community, the *Visitatio Sepulchri* was close to ritual. The greatest development of the new tradition took place outside the church. Sponsored by Christian laymen, the liturgical plays developed into the miracle or mystery plays, performed in the vernacular with much spectacle on the feast of Corpus Christi by members of the guilds of the towns which grew and prospered in the late Middle Ages. Drawing their material from the Bible, these told the story of the creation and the fall and redemption of man. There were other plays which dealt with the legends of the saints. A quite different genre was the morality play, more concerned with the direct preaching of the Christian message, and employing symbolism to bring the message home to the spectators.

This association of drama with religion is one of the reasons for the long series of prohibitions laid upon drama: the forbidding, in Deuteronomy, of the exchange of clothes between the sexes, originally directed against some pagan dramatic ritual and invoked by Zeal-of-the-land Busy in *Bartholomew Fair*; the excommunication of actors in fourth-century Rome and in seventeenth-century France, where Molière was at first refused Christian burial; the banning of the Catholic miracle plays by the Reformed Church in the sixteenth century; the Catholic and Protestant suppression of folk plays and rituals; the long Puritan and Nonconformist attacks on the stage; Marxist censorship. In all of these instances, the drama is involved in the struggle between one system of belief and another.

The State and the Drama

The performance of a Greek play was a state occasion, attended by civic leaders and foreign ambassadors. The costs were borne by public-spirited citizens or came from public funds. In the fifth century, the tragedies of Aeschylus, Sophocles and Euripides and the comedies of Aristophanes handled great political, social and moral issues. It is only very exceptionally, however, that we find a government with sufficient faith in the drama and democracy to allow such freedom of expression, let alone sponsor it. Political tensions already began to curb the freedom of Aristophanes in his later comedies, and, a century later, Menander, in his so-called 'new comedy', had to confine himself to non-political domestic stories. It is not until we come to the Reformation and the freedom created by the balance of power between opposing parties, that we again find the drama discussing great issues confronting nations, but only in a partisan spirit. The established morality form lent itself admirably to this function. The most striking example is Sir David Lindsay's *Satire of The Three Estates*, which, when it was performed in Edinburgh in 1554, was paid for by the Corporation and presented before the Queen Regent and a great assembly of lords and commons. This reappearance of a political drama was short-lived. In Scotland, the Reformed Kirk, strongly influenced by English Puritanism, was powerful enough to put an end to dramatic performances. In England, where, by the Act of 1572, players could incur the penalties of the law as 'rogues and vagabonds', Queen Elizabeth stood between the players and the Puritans; but her government, by various legal enactments, ensured that the drama should not call in question either the established church or government policy, a course which, in any case, playwrights and theatrical companies became less and less likely to follow, since they were increasingly dependent on a court audience. All the English companies were required by law to serve under a noble patron, and, under James I, the company of which Shakespeare was a member became 'the King's Men' and could be regarded as the first national theatre company. The theatres were closed by Parliament in 1642, and the ban continued throughout the Commonwealth period. At the Restoration, the King granted patents for two theatres and two companies, one of which was established under his own patronage, the other under the Duke of York's, continuing the association of the drama with the court. It was not until the 1720s and 1730s, with the *Beggar's Opera* and the satirical plays of Fielding, that there was again an openly political theatre in England. It was short-lived, for it provoked Walpole into bringing in his Licensing Act of 1737, establishing the system of censorship by the Lord Chamberlain, which turned Fielding from the drama to the novel and discouraged serious writers from writing for the theatre for a century and a half. It was only after a prolonged campaign, beginning with Shaw and the Ibsenites in the 1880s and 1890s, that the Licensing Act was finally replaced by the Theatres Act of 1968.

The 1737 Act also confirmed the two-theatre system established by Charles II, the patents now being held by Covent

Garden and Drury Lane. This system continued in force until 1843. It was by reason of their privileged position that Drury Lane and Covent Garden, the two 'major' houses, grew to their enormous dimensions as compared with other London theatres. Even when enlarged, however, these two theatres could not meet the demands for entertainment of the vastly increased population of London in the early nineteenth century. Other 'minor' theatres sprang up, but as they were prevented by law from presenting regular plays, they had to turn to melodrama, originally just a play accompanied by music, as the derivation shows.

If we bear in mind that the drama could have a religious and social as well as an artistic function, we shall see that the student of the history of the drama must look beyond plays and books about the theatre for his material. For the study of the origins of the drama, Sir James Fraser's classic of anthropology, *The Golden Bough*, is essential reading. Other important sources of theatre history are ecclesiastical records and devotional and moralizing works. Again, an immense amount of material is located in proclamations, ordinances, Acts, parliamentary papers and the records of government departments and of local authorities.

Government interest in the drama should not be thought of as entirely restrictive. The terms of the patents granted by Charles II recognized the moral and intellectual importance of drama. The patent theatres proudly bore the title 'Royal'. In the later eighteenth and early nineteenth centuries, most towns of any importance successfully petitioned for the right to establish theatres royal. These patents, while they conferred a monopoly on managements, also required from them a service to art and to the public. A later recognition by authority of the social value of the drama was the conferring of knighthoods upon distinguished men of the theatre, the first actor to be knighted being Henry Irving in 1895. It was not until the Second World War that the government began to give direct financial aid to the theatre. The establishment of the Arts Council and of a Ministry for the Arts marks a return to the attitudes of Greek civilization, when the provision of drama was regarded as a legitimate object of public expenditure.

One of the most important areas of government action

affecting the theatre is copyright. It was not until the 1860s that the establishment of dramatic copyright protected a writer's interest in his work, and then it only applied to performances in this country.

A government's responsibility for ensuring proper conditions of employment must extend to the theatre. Throughout the seventeenth and eighteenth centuries, actors, being 'His Majesty's servants', had a right to appeal to the Lord Chamberlain for redress of complaints against managements. Towards the end of the nineteenth century, legislation was brought in to control the employment of children in the theatre.

A government is also responsible for the maintenance of public order and for the health and safety of the public. In Elizabethan times we find that the theatres were closed when the plague was rife. Disastrous theatre fires, so frequent in the early nineteenth century, were greatly reduced in number in the second half of the century by the introduction of strict fire regulations.

The Economic History of the Theatre

Even when one considers purely theatrical matters, these do not all fall into the category of art. There is an economic side of the theatre. As phrases like 'show business' and 'bricks and mortar' indicate, drama is an art which calls for resources in capital, in materials and in personnel. Its scope and character have been shaped by the economic forces of society, and its organization has reflected the stage of economic development of society. The first professional companies, each consisting only of three or four players, emerged in the later Middle Ages as retainers of a feudal lord. The first economically independent companies (which were still nominally the servants of a lord) were small units of only a few actors. They could only please audiences accustomed to the large amateur casts of the miracle plays by commissioning plays which permitted a great deal of doubling of parts, like Marlowe's *Tamburlaine*. These companies were owned by certain of the actors, who, as 'sharers', held the capital of the company, consisting of costumes, properties and plays, in common, and hired the other adult members of the company, while the boy actors, who played

C

women's parts, were apprenticed to an individual actor. The companies prospered and recruited more members, until what they demanded from the playwright was the typical Jacobean play with its large cast of mature actors, which few managements can afford to stage today. The capitalist first made his appearance as the owner of the theatre in which these companies played, the first theatre being built by James Burbage in 1576. Towards the end of the seventeenth century, the capitalist, in the person of the manager, began to take over the financing of the company as well as of the theatre, the actors becoming merely employees. This system worked best when the manager was also the leading actor. The era of the actor-managers extended from the eighteenth century – with David Garrick – through the nineteenth century – with John Philip Kemble, William Macready, Charles Kean, Samuel Phelps, Henry Irving, George Alexander – to the twentieth century – with Forbes Robinson, Benson, and the last of the great actor-managers, Sir Donald Wolfit. The typical Victorian actor-manager bore a marked similarity to the paternalist Victorian industrialist. Again, the economic factor had a bearing on the plays, which, whether original works or versions of classics, had to be vehicles for the talents of the actor-manager.

In the mixed economy of mid-twentieth-century Britain, we have, side by side, the commercial, privately-owned theatre and the state-subsidized theatre, which is usually organized as a non-profit-making company administered by a non-professional board of directors. An actors' trade union, Equity, was founded in 1929.

Whatever the system of economic organization, a theatre can be run efficiently or inefficiently, a factor which has affected the course of theatre history. How is the efficiency of an artistic enterprise to be judged, however? A box-office success or a more efficient method of economic organization may be undesirable from the point of view of art. For example, in the mid-nineteenth century, the costly permanent ('stock') company, with its repertory of plays, was superseded by the company recruited to present one play performed continuously until its drawing power was exhausted – the present 'long-run' system. Today, both the National Theatre and the Royal Shakespeare Company have revived the repertory system (which, of course, never went out of use for ballet or opera), believing it to provide better conditions for the actor to develop his art. Again, the building of railways in the nineteenth century made it cheaper to send out a London-based company than to maintain provincial stock companies, which became extinct. Today, the repertory theatre movement is an attempt to revive them.

Theatrical Audiences

The history of the theatre has often been told in terms of its audience. Theoretically, at least, other artists can stop at self-expression, at writing or painting to please themselves. 'Fit audience find, though few' is a possible ambition for a poet, but not for a playwright or a player. One can think of important poets whose work was neglected, even unpublished in their own lifetime, but every important playwright has had some measure of contemporary theatrical success, while an actor, being a performer, cannot exist without someone to perform to. The drama is an expensive art form and must please a large number of people who are prepared to pay for their pleasure, either directly at the box office or indirectly through taxation. The importance of the audience is, however, not only, or indeed mainly, economic. Drama, unlike many arts, has preserved its social character. Reading a play may provide an unforgettable aesthetic experience, but it is clearly something different in kind from being present at a performance. It is like reading a poem or a novel: there is nothing specifically dramatic about it. In a sense, a play only exists when it is being acted before an audience. The playwright builds audience reaction into his play; the producer and designer try to see their work through the eyes of the audience, metaphorically and indeed literally, as they move from one part of the house to another during rehearsals. The theatre has been planned by the architect to comply with an estimate of the audience which will patronize it. How much more this involvement with the audience must matter to the actors who are in direct contact with them! The actor interprets the play afresh for each night's audience. He must receive an impetus from his audience if he is to give his best. For the great actor, every performance is 'one-off'. It is this special relationship which explains the importance of applause, which may seem a tedious custom to those who lack this sense that every performance is an occasion.

Sufficient material exists from the Elizabethan period onwards for the history of theatre audiences to be investigated in some detail. It has been shown that Elizabethan 'public' theatres like Shakespeare's Globe catered for a wide audience, extending from the aristocracy to intellectuals and educated working men, an audience which liked plays which dealt with matters which concerned everybody, and where the treatment was bold in outline and rich in detail. The so-called 'private theatres', like the Blackfriars Theatre where Shakespeare's company began to play in the winter months after 1609, had higher prices and drew a socially more exclusive audience. Any gain in artistic sophistication was offset by a certain neglect of fundamental human values. The court masques of the reigns of James I and Charles I temporarily diverted a great deal of the available theatrical resources entirely into the service of the court. A brilliant assemblage of talent in writing, design, music and dance was devoted to a sort of apotheosis of the king, who received this homage seated on a throne in a commanding position in the audience. Meanwhile, certain public playhouses began to cater for the popular audience with vulgarizations of older plays, especially those which had plenty of noisy action in them, like *Dr Faustus* with its devils running about the stage. This is the beginning of a division in the audience which has lasted until the present day, to the great impoverishment of our drama.

The overthrow of the Monarchy by the Commonwealth meant the overthrow of the theatre. When theatres opened again at the Restoration, even if the audiences were less exclusively drawn from the aristocracy than was once thought, the whole tone of the theatre was set by the Court. Charles II went frequently to the theatre, which no monarch had done before. Two of his mistresses, Nell Gwynn and Moll Davis, were actresses, and Restoration comedy has for its subject-matter the life of a pleasure-loving society which valued wit and beauty. The contrasting serious drama of the period, the 'heroic play' with its romanticized treatment of honour and love, can perhaps be explained as appealing to the nostalgia for the past of an aristocracy which was losing its political and economic precedence.

By the end of the seventeenth century, the rising mercantile class began to influence theatrical taste. This was observed by the contemporary writer John Dennis:

> In the Reign of King Charles the Second, a considerable part of an Audience had that due application, which is requisite for the judging of Comedy. They had first of all leisure to attend to it. For that was an age of Pleasure, and not of Business. They were serene enough to receive its impressions: for they were in Ease and Plenty. But in the present Reign, a great part of the Gentlemen have not leisure, because want throws them upon employments, and there are ten times more Gentlemen now in business, than there were in King Charles his Reign. Nor have they serenity, by Reason of a War [War of the Spanish Succession, 1701–1714], in which all are concerned, by reason of the Taxes which make them uneasie. . . . They come to a Playhouse full of some business which they have been solliciting, or of some Harrangue which they are to make the next day; so that they meerly come to unbend.

The danger of over-simplifying the influence of an audience on the drama is shown by the fact that the call for theatrical reform came not from a middle-class moralist, but from a Tory High Churchman, Jeremy Collier, in his *Short View of the Immorality and Profaneness of the English Stage* (1698).

This occasion does not afford space to discuss the cross-currents of taste in the eighteenth century, but if we move on to the early nineteenth century, we can see another difficulty of relating audience and play. One tends to assume a direct relationship, that the play will reflect the lives of the audience, will 'hold the mirror up to nature'. It is clear from the evidence of the early-nineteenth-century theatre, however, that this need not be a direct reflection. The social and economic status of the new audiences which crowded into the theatres of the early nineteenth century – the era of the Industrial Revolution – has not yet been thoroughly investigated, and of course it would vary between major and minor theatres, but it is certain that many of these theatre-goers were poor and living in bad housing conditions. An early-nineteenth-century evangelist defended his venture of holding Sunday Services in a theatre instead of urging his hearers to go to church, by pointing out that those who would go to the theatre could not afford the decent clothes expected of church-goers. When a false alarm of fire caused a riot in the Theatre Royal, Glasgow, in 1849, the money found in the pockets of the sixty-five victims amounted to a total of only 17s. 1d. It is evident that the lives of the audiences bore no direct resemblance to the daring deeds and exotic settings of the plays they saw. It is too easy to give the answer that this was an escapist theatre of mere entertainment. One cannot square this with the vigour of the campaign led by churchmen, especially Nonconformists, against the theatre. The claims of the moral and social value of the theatre made by its supporters might be dismissed as partial, but not the fact that its opponents thought it a force to be reckoned with. One is reminded of the discussion today of the effects of television. Perhaps what these audiences saw on the stage – being figures and scenes from an inner life of their fantasies and dreams – was as real to them as the actual social circumstances would have been.

The early nineteenth century exemplifies, in an extreme form, the social division in audiences which began, as we have seen, with the Elizabethan 'private' theatre. Repelled by the popular audience and its taste, the upper classes and serious writers of the second quarter of the century had, to a great extent, withdrawn their regular support from the theatre, and went to the opera instead. The meeting of any actual audience-demand was not possible, however, until the law confining the legitimate drama to the patent theatres was altered in 1843. Thereafter, actor-managers like Charles Kean and Irving could present plays in smaller theatres, where a more subtle style of acting was possible. Here it may be observed that the influence of an audience is affected by the way in which it is disposed in the auditorium, and an important innovation of the mid-nineteenth century was a change in the seating and in the prices of the area most closely in contact with the stage. The pit, moderately priced and socially mixed, was replaced by the expensive stalls, so that the upper-class element in the audience was given a dominant position. If Charles Kean and Irving managed to some extent to appeal to all classes, their achievement was the exception. In 1865 the management of the Bancrofts at the Prince of Wales Theatre introduced the comparative realism of Thomas Robertson's plays, a genre continued by Henry Arthur Jones, Arthur Pinero and Oscar Wilde. The upper classes were drawn back to the theatre by plays in which manners, clothes, furnishings and values in question were their own. As the drawing room 'cup and saucer' drama evolved at one end of the social scale, at the other end music hall flourished.

Still later in the century, the long estrangement between the intelligentsia and the theatre seemed to be at an end when, beginning with special performances in London organized by the Independent Theatre and the Stage Society, something like a modern *avant-garde* movement made its appearance. This movement led to the Vedrenne–Granville Barker management at the Court from 1904 to 1907, and, out of London, to the first of the so called 'repertory theatres': in Dublin (the Abbey), Manchester, Glasgow, Liverpool and Birmingham.

The nineteenth century could therefore be said to have bequeathed to the twentieth a taste for the theatre in all classes, but unfortunately the classes were divided into three separate audiences – the popular audience, the upper classes and the intellectuals. The popular audience, as far as regular support went, was soon to be lost to the cinema, which inherited many of the traditions of melodrama and music hall. The cinema, however, has been much more successful than the drama in appealing to all three audiences. Indeed, it could be claimed that it has rediscovered the secret of the universal appeal of the Elizabethan public theatre.

If the full history of theatre audience is ever to be written, it will have to go beyond the level on which we have discussed the matter so far. It is no doubt valuable, up to a point, to discuss a class and its likes and dislikes, to consider a play and its appeal, as if we were dealing with the supply and demand of objects. We have to remember, however, the subjective nature of the theatrical experience, and it is clear that this is not the same at all places and times or, indeed, for every member of the audience. In fact, before we can write a history of theatrical audiences, we need a historical study of audience psychology.

The early-nineteenth-century audience behaved in a way

quite unlike any theatre audience today, although it was perhaps like the modern pop music audience, as we can see from this quotation from Charles Lamb:

> Damn 'em, how they hissed! It was not a hiss, neither, but a sort of frantic yell like a congregation of wild geese, with roaring, sometimes, like bears, mows and mops like apes, sometimes snakes that hissed me into madness. 'T was like St. Anthony's temptations. Mercy on us that God should give his favourite children, men, mouths to speak with, to discourse rationally, to promise smoothly, to flatter agreeably, to encourage warmly, to counsel wisely, to sing with, to drink with, and to kiss with, and that they should turn them into mouths of adders, bears, wolves, hyenas, and whistle like tempests, and emit breath through them like distillations and aspic poisons, to asperse and vilify the innocent labours of their fellow-creatures who are desirous to please them.

If it could damn a play with such vehemence, this audience could respond with equal energy to a performance which held them. One thinks of ladies fainting when Edmund Kean as Sir Giles Overreach came on as an armed madman. (This sort of effect could be achieved even outside of the theatre: there is the episode of Mrs Siddons at Portpatrick in Scotland, where she was waiting to embark for Ireland, speaking a few appropriate lines from one of her parts, with a wild cry, and inducing a kind of primitive panic in the villagers.) It was an impressionable age then, when audiences went to the theatre expecting to be deeply affected, as one might go to a Revivalist meeting, and to that extent they were willing subjects for a theatrical spellbinder. On the other hand, it could be that actors and audiences together created powerful theatrical images which can now only be faintly imagined. This would explain the paradox of the nineteenth-century theatre – the contrast between the deep impression it made on its audiences and the triviality of the plays judged as literature. The classic example is Irving's performances as Matthias in *The Bells*. The text is pedestrian, even absurd, and yet we must believe, on the evidence not only of popular success, but also on the testimony of discriminating men of letters, that Irving made of the part an unforgettable image of the deepest contradictions of our common humanity.

The Performing Arts

So far we have been considering the history of the arts of the
theatre in their social context. When we come to consider the
history of the arts themselves, we are faced with the problem of
drawing the bounds of theatre. Is it to be distinguished from
closely associated activities, and, if so, what is the distinguishing
feature?

Theatre is sometimes detached from the wider field of art and
entertainment as a performing art, that is, an art which is
presented to the audience by a performer. Thus, theatre is
grouped with music, dance, circus and so on. It is more difficult
to distinguish theatre from the other performing arts than
might at first appear. Nor should this really prove surprising,
for in the beginning they were one. The Greek drama still
preserved its chorus which sang and danced, but also took part
in the dialogue and action of the play. The oriental drama, even
in its later forms like Japanese *kabuki* (literally, 'singing-
dancing-acting') and Chinese Peking Opera, also keeps the
original unity. The history of the theatre is the history of the
divergence of the originally allied arts, a divergence which is
periodically arrested by attempts to restore the alliance, as in
the masque, opera and modern experiments in mixed media.

The musician is hardly a performer in the same sense as the
others, in that what he is performing is the music, while what
they are offering to the audience is themselves. But there is a
further difference between the circus performer, on the one
hand and the actor on the other: though both offer themselves
to the audience – the young man on the flying trapeze offers
his real daring, whereas the actor offers himself in order to
show the stage hero's imaginary daring. It is the actor's imper-
sonation which has defined the course of theatre history.

The opera singer is an obvious exception to the generaliza-
tion about musicians, and the theatre historian must include
opera in his province. Of the circus performers, the clown
belongs to theatre history. In the nineteenth century, certain
circuses, of which the most famous was Astley's, turned their
special skills to dramatic account in 'hippodramas' – plays

introducing spectacular equestrian feats. (The principle was the same as that of the ice show, which will no doubt one day be written up by a theatre historian.) The dancer occupies an intermediate position between the actor and the acrobat, but in so far as he creates a character, as in ballet, he too is part of theatre history. The music hall artists can qualify in the same way. Puppetry is a form of theatre with a long and varied history which must include the Japanese *bunraku*, with its almost life-size puppets, and the widespread shadow-plays.

A twentieth-century extension of the subject is film history, which in some respects has been better covered than the theatre of the same period. The other contemporary developments of radio and television are as yet almost unexplored.

Theatre Arts: Acting

The actor may take precedence among the artists of the theatre, but his art is ephemeral as compared with that of the playwright, who provides his text, or the architect, who provides him with a theatre to play in.

We know more about the masks and costumes of the classical theatre than about the actor who wore them. The name of Roscius has passed into the language as a synonym for a great actor, but there are no records which enable us to picture his acting style. As for the theatre in Britain, the history of acting can only be written in any detail from the mid-eighteenth century onwards, that is to say, it begins with Garrick.

The records which have survived from the previous four centuries afford us an increasingly clear picture of the lives of actors, less so of their art. One early document, dating from the beginning of the fifteenth century, is an actor's part in three liturgical plays which employed both Latin and English. The part contains just the one actor's lines, introduced by his cues. From guild records we know the names of the amateurs who took part in miracle plays, what they were paid and something of their rehearsal schedules. The famous stage direction 'Here Herod rages in the pageant' (that is, the stage of the street theatre) 'and in the street also' indicates a larger-than-life performance, but it was no doubt intended to be half comic. Other stage directions call for the actor's making his meaning plain by illustrative rather than realistic gestures, as when John is told to point to Jesus with his finger when speaking the line 'Ecce agnus dei' ('Behold the lamb of God'). Though the longer expository, lyrical and rhetorical passages would require special techniques of elocution and gesture, action seems to have been comparatively naturalistic. 'Here shall a messenger come into the place, running and crying "Tidings, tidings", and so round about the place "Jesus of Nazareth is taken, Jesus of Nazareth is taken".' Particularly striking are passages like the nailing of Christ to the cross in the York Crucifixion, where the four soldiers have to carry out the horrible and difficult stage business while speaking individual lines and half-lines which combine to make an elaborate rhyming stanza.

Minstrels and other professional performers had existed throughout the Middle Ages, and the first professional actors were very likely recruited from them. The first professional actors known are a company of six in the service of Richard III, which seems appropriate in view of his later success as a Shakespearean role. The companies remained small – perhaps three men and a boy to play the women's parts – until the great Elizabethan theatre boom which followed upon the opening of the first playhouses in the late 1570s. There are portraits of three of the most celebrated Elizabethan actors, and we can see the commanding presence of Edmund Alleyn, who played Marlowe's Tamburlaine; the sensitive eyes of Richard Burbage, who created Shakespeare's greatest roles; and the almost too perfect good looks of Nathan Field. None of these are theatrical portraits, however; and the majority of the references to them – which do not go beyond general praise – do not help us to see them in a particular part. It is only exceptionally that the veil is lifted from the past, and through the eyes of a contemporary we suddenly see Burbage as Hamlet leaping into Ophelia's grave:

> Oft have I seen him leap into the grave,
> Suiting the person that he seemed to have
> Of a sad lover with so true an eye,
> That there I would have sworn, he meant to die.

The liveliness of this description seems to argue against the theory that the Elizabethan acting style was formal. Perhaps,

as has also been argued, there were two styles: a more declama-
tory, heroic style, of which Alleyn, at his best in a 'majestic'
part, was the great master; and a more naturalistic style
developed by Burbage, who, playing the part of Hamlet, advised actors to 'speak trippingly on the tongue'. It seems more
likely that any successful actor of the period must have been the
master of a style of unusual range, extending from naturalism
to the delivery and gesture of the rhetorician. It does not really
clinch the matter to produce a contemporary reference to
Burbage's 'wholly transforming himself into his part', for the
same has been said of the great actors (even of the great
dancers) of every age. What we need to know is the means by
which Burbage conveyed this transformation to his audience.
Still another problem is how the Elizabethan actor maintained
contact with the audience which surrounded him on three sides.
Again, we do not know how the boy actors played the women's
parts. In the present state of knowledge, it seems that Elizabethan acting is something of a lost art.

By the Restoration, we are in the age of biographies and
theatrical portraits, and one would think that with the fame of
the great actor Thomas Betterton and the impact of the
actresses, who then ousted the boy actors, one would at last be
able to speak of acting styles with some confidence, but the
evidence is still open to more than one interpretation. Even the
first classic of English theatrical literature, Cibber's *Apology*,
of 1740, with its lively reminiscences of actors and actresses of
the turn of the century, is still very general in what it tells us.
One thing that can be said, on the evidence of the portraits, is
that the interpretation of character in Restoration comedies
seems to have been much less eccentric than it usually is when
they are revived today. Tragic acting, on the other hand,
especially in the early eighteenth century, seems to have shown
a taste for what was called 'tone', a sort of chanting delivery.

By the time Garrick made his debut in 1741, sources of
information expanded to such a point that we can now know
how the actor spoke certain lines and what his gestures were.
Works on the theory of acting, making reference to contemporary practice, began to appear; and literary men, like Charles
Churchill in his *Rosciad* (1761), devoted poems to the review
of the talents of contemporary actors. The theatrical critic had

made his appearance, though for theatrical criticism as we know it today we have to wait for Leigh Hunt and Hazlitt at the beginning of the next century. Theatre-goers made detailed notes of how Garrick played his big scenes, and we have some idea both of the motivation he gave to the characters he played and of the means by which he communicated their inner life to the audience. We can appreciate, even at this remove, something of the intensity of feeling which he brought to a part and the heightened naturalism by which he expressed it.

Thereafter we can trace the changes in acting style through the well-documented careers of John Philip Kemble and his sister Mrs Siddons, Edmund Kean and Charles Kean, Macready and Irving to the advent of naturalism, which still dominates the theatre, despite the *avant-garde* under the influence of Brecht and the Polish director, Jerzy Grotowski.

Closely allied with the history of acting is the history of the actor's masks or make-up and of stage costume.

Theatre Arts: Architecture

The actor may first have performed in a shrine or a church, a place which enforced belief in the ritual drama but was not necessarily suitable otherwise for a performance. The need to be seen and heard was met in two ways. The audience could be arranged in a circle round the acting area: this was the task of the Presenter of the Mummers' Play who entered first with his cry of 'Room!'; and it was also the arrangement of the early Greek theatres, where all the action took place on the level circular orchestra and the surrounding audience was accommodated on staging or on seats on a hillside. The other method, also of great antiquity, for it is shown in Greek vase paintings, is to raise the actor on a stage. Of course, both methods can be combined, as they were in the fully developed Greek theatre.

To judge by a diagram in the manuscript of *The Castle of Perseverance*, the mediaeval audience sometimes formed a circle around the acting area, which was a level piece of ground with a few stages or 'scaffolds' erected on it, each stage providing a setting for a particular episode or episodes, though the actors used the ground as well. The miracle plays were commonly acted in the streets on 'pageants' (high stages mounted on wheels). The mobility of the pageants allowed the plays to be repeated in different parts of the town. The first professional companies played mostly in the halls of great houses, similar to the college halls of Oxford and Cambridge. It is one of the great paradoxes of English theatrical history that although our familiarity with the plays that Shakespeare wrote is so great, our knowledge of the theatres in which Shakespeare's plays were performed is so imperfect. We do know, however, that these theatres were open to the sky and that the main acting area was a large roofed platform extending to the middle of the auditorium, an arrangement which, with the provision of tiers of balconies, made it possible to accommodate a large audience without any member of it being remote from the stage. The form of the Swan theatre, the Dutch traveller John De Witt noted, 'resembles a Roman work'; but the auditorium was also derived from buildings used for other forms of entertainment (indeed, as we know from *Bartholomew Fair*, the Hope play-house was also used for bear-baiting), and the stage arrangements derived from the accumulated theatrical experience of the Middle Ages.

Perspective scenery came into use in public theatres at the time of the Restoration. This called for a new design of theatre, with a deep stage, to accommodate the receding planes of scenery and a proscenium arch, to frame the picture. Until the nineteenth century, a vestige of the Elizabethan platform continued to exist in the form of an apron entered by stage doors in front of the proscenium. The taste for naturalism finally led to its disappearance, and the actors retreated to their mimic world which the spectator observed through an invisible fourth wall indicated by the proscenium.

The proscenium arch was soon to be filled by a cinema screen. This is no doubt one of the reasons why the theatre in the twentieth century has been in search of its identity, a search which has led to the revival of historical forms of theatre: the thrust stage and theatre-in-the-round.

Theatre Arts: Scenery and Lighting

We never ask where the combat of the Mummers' Play is

supposed to happen. Usually, however, the action of a play is provided with a setting, though this may be rather vague. The ways of indicating the place of the action have varied throughout theatrical history. In the *Visitatio Sepulchri* the tomb was indicated by the 'Easter sepulchre', a niche in the altar or in the inside wall of the church at the choir. It was an emblematic rather than a realistic representation of a tomb. In later versions of the play, a scene was added in which the women bought spices with which to anoint the body of Jesus. For this episode a second setting, of a merchant's booth, was provided. When the scene changed from the booth to the tomb the women merely moved from the first setting to the second. The fully developed mediaeval drama retained this method which is known as multiple staging or *décor simultané*, since all the settings were simultaneously present throughout the play. Moreover, though the miracle plays could achieve spectacular effects, sometimes involving the use of stage machinery, their scenery continued to be emblematic rather than realistic; for example, a large canopy supported by pillars, with a throne, would serve for Herod's Palace.

In the Elizabethan public theatres, settings could be indicated by set pieces; for example, Hieronymo's garden in *The Spanish Tragedy* is indicated by the bower from which his son Horatio is hanged. The method, however, seems rather to have been for the actor to create his own setting, helped by the permanent features of the stage, so that the gallery over the stage could serve as the battlements of Flint Castle or of Harfleur. Perhaps it was the fact that the actor created his own setting which enabled these theatres to dispense with *décor simultané*.

Perspective scenery, that is, scenery which employs perspective, as in painting, to give an illusion of three dimensions to a two-dimensional surface, was invented in Italy and first introduced into England by Inigo Jones in the Court masques of the reigns of James I and Charles I. Many of Jones's designs and plans survive: we can see that after a period of experimentation he evolved a method of changing scenes by sliding flats on and off stage, and this method survived until the nineteenth century, when scenery came to be flown, that is, raised and lowered, a technical improvement rather than a change in basic principle.

Perspective scenery was illusionist and incompatible with the convention of *décor simultané*; besides, it was now technically possible to provide a succession of settings as the action moved from place to place.

'The friezes, both below and above, were filled with several coloured lights like emeralds, rubies, carbuncles, etc., the reflex of which . . . upon the masquers' habits was full of glory,' wrote Jonson of Jones's design for the House of Fame in *The Masque of Queens*. With Jones and the move to indoor theatres, lighting, which had always been an important consideration in theatre planning, for the actor must always be in the light, first assumed artistic importance. The light sources available to Jones – candles and oil lamps – were, of course, technically limited.

While reflecting the changes in taste in the visual arts – and so passing from the classical symmetry of Jones's designs, through the baroque, followed by the romanticism of Garrick's designer De Loutherbourg, to the picturesque historical painting of the great Victorian scenic artist – perspective scenery was always spectacular and placed the designer almost on a level with the playwright and actor. The introduction of scenery created difficulties in Shakespearian productions: scenes in his plays had to be rearranged because nineteenth-century stage machinery could not keep pace with the rapid scene changes which the Elizabethan theatre made possible. Moreover, in Shakespeare's theatre, the balance of picture and word was different.

Perspective scenery gave an illusion of three dimensions, but hardly so as to deceive. It fell into disfavour with the growth of the general demand for realism in the arts in the later nineteenth century and was replaced by the three-dimensional box set which matched the new realistic player.

Its value was also challenged by the revolutionary ideas of Gordon Craig. The typical Craig design replaced painted flats and cloths by simple three-dimensional forms – columns, steps, rostra, draped curtains – or by the essential furniture required by the action, set against a cyclorama. In his view, the flexibility of electric lighting rendered scene painting, with its unchangeable colour and chiaroscuro, obsolete (gas lighting had been introduced in the early nineteenth century, but its artistic possibilities were not fully exploited, except perhaps by Irving).

The scene designer today also works under the influence of William Poel, who experimented in reviving Elizabethan staging, and of Brecht, whose idea of alienation was directed against spectacular or realistic scenery, since it would contribute to a total involvement of the spectators in the play, whereas he wanted them to retain sufficient detachment for them to think about its message.

Theatre Arts: Directing

The producer or director first made his appearance in the late nineteenth century. It was his task to coordinate all the artistic elements in a production. Though the post was new, the concern for ensemble was not, and the task had, at various times in the past, been the responsibility of the writer, the leading actor or the stage manager. It is ironical that the director, appointed to unite playwright, actors and designer in a common effort, should himself have become the 'creative director', still another artist seeking to dominate the production. It is a disturbing reflection on twentieth-century English theatre that the two greatest directors, Granville-Barker (who saw his task as being to serve the author's text) and Gordon Craig (who thought of the director as the creator of a new art of the theatre), should both have abandoned the practice of the theatre in their prime.

Future Research

At a time when research is going forward in all periods, stimulated by the establishment of university departments of drama and of The Society for Theatre Research, it is difficult to select areas attracting particular interest. I suppose, however, that some areas can be picked out because of their importance, or because they have been neglected or because they have a contemporary relevance.

In view of the pre-eminence of Shakespeare, it is natural that the period of theatre history which has attracted most attention is the Elizabethan. This vast effort of scholarship has established almost everything about the Elizabethan playhouse except what

D

we most want to know: the stage arrangements. It was in 1888 that the De Witt drawing of the Swan came to light, the only picture we have of the interior of an Elizabethan public play-house, and unfortunately this picture is difficult to interpret. It may be that another sketch is waiting discovery. In the mean-time, the question is so important that it will continue to engage scholars, whether they try to answer it by a re-examination of the circumstantial evidence or by practical experiment.

After being regarded as of mainly philological interest, the mediaeval drama has been reappraised by theatre historians during the past twenty years. Only now are we beginning to see it as comparable with other artistic achievements of the Middle Ages.

Another neglected area, as I have already indicated, is nineteenth-century theatre. Here again there is a revaluation in progress. We have too long looked at early nineteenth-century theatre through the eyes of the realists who were in reaction against it.

I suspect that the interest in these three subjects is not due just to their importance or to their having been neglected, but also to the fact that they are felt to have some relevance to the contemporary situation, when the theatre is trying to find itself again, to rediscover its social function, its audience, its true nature as an art. Here, two other areas of historical study come to mind: national and regional theatre; and the political theatre of the early eighteenth century.

Finally, though the policy has been to confine this chapter, as far as possible, to British theatre history, one cannot shut out the fact that theatre is an art that readily passes national boun-daries, and that there is even felt to be a contemporary rele-vance in the study of oriental drama.

The Drama and History in General

This chapter has dealt only with theatre history, but it should be borne in mind that other branches of history are also of great value to the student of drama. Social history in all its aspects, including special studies like the history of costume and of etiquette, is extremely valuable. The actors who play Adam and Orlando in *As You Like It*, or the actresses who play Olga,

Natasha and Anfisa in *Three Sisters*, must embody social attitudes which mark the end of a feudal system. In *The Spanish Tragedy*, the relative positions on the stage of the members of the royal family on the one hand and of Hieronimo and Horatio on the other indicate the existence of a caste system, on which the motivation of the play depends. A particularly effective use of historical knowledge was the revival, in the Gielgud production of *Hamlet* in 1936, of the original method of duelling employing rapier and dagger. In comedy, which tends to be more topical than tragedy, historical knowledge is of particular importance. Of a 'breeches' part, in which Nell Gwynn played a 'young gallant', Pepys writes, 'she hath the motions and carriage of a spark, the most that ever I saw any man have. It makes me, I confess, admire her.' In her lines, Nell Gwynn speaks of combing her hair, and a contemporary work, *The Young Gallant's Academy*, gives us a hint of how this might be done. For at least two centuries, playwrights could assume that their actresses would understand the language of the fan. The Osric episode in Hamlet requires knowledge of when to wear one's hat and of the significance of having a feather in it. For the plays of Jones, Pinero and Wilde, the Du Maurier drawings in Punch are an inspiring source of information.

Also of the greatest importance is art history. In the nineteenth century, the antiquarian style prevailed in Shakespearian production. Charles Kean, the actor-manager, was a Fellow of the Society of Antiquaries. The designer William Capon was also an authority on the history of architecture. E. W. Godwin, the father of Gordon Craig, designed a *Merchant of Venice* in which the scenery was inspired by his analysis of the stylistic development of Venetian architecture. Later designers have been less bound by purely antiquarian considerations. Komisarjevsky's *Antony and Cleopatra*, for example, was an attempt to recreate on the stage, not Rome, but rather the Renaissance idea of Rome, and drew its inspiration from the paintings of Veronese. An extreme case is the ballet *The Rake's Progress*, which was, in fact, inspired by a work of art, Hogarth's series of engravings of that title.

Producers and other designers have felt free to disregard both the date at which the events of the play are supposed to take place and the date at which the play was composed, and to set it in a period which might seem to them either more decorative or, in some way, more expressive of their interpretation of the play than either of these alternatives. The recent National Theatre production of *Love's Labour's Lost* was clearly inspired by illuminations of a mediaeval manuscript, the *Très Riches Heures du Duc de Berry*. The current National Theatre *Merchant of Venice* moves the play forward from the sixteenth century to the 1880s.

Drama uses not only words but also a second language of theatrical conventions and social modes, the dictionary of which is history.

2

Plays

Kenneth Muir

Every year a large number of new plays are produced in the West End or on Broadway, and many of them are taken off after a few performances. They have been read by experienced men of the theatre, produced by experienced directors, and performed by experienced actors; yet, when it comes to the point, audiences and critics condemn the plays. Sometimes this may be due to miscasting or a mistake of the producer; sometimes the play may offend some deep-rooted prejudice or puzzle by its originality – as Chekhov's plays did when they were first performed in England – but more often than not it is the play itself that turns out to be bad. On the other hand, one of the great successes of the inter-war period, R. C. Sherriff's *Journey's End*, was rejected by every well-known London management; and Bernard Shaw's early plays were all rejected by the commercial theatres. These points illustrate how difficult it is, even for experienced and intelligent people, to judge the value of a play merely by reading the text; and to train students to read plays more successfully is one of the functions of a department of drama.

It is often said that there are three kinds of theatre – actors', directors' and authors' – and certainly one can have a theatre in which a great actor makes a huge success of plays which have no permanent value – Irving's performance in *The Bells* is a stock example. Sometimes, too, a great producer, subordinating a play and its cast to some idea of his own, can provide us with an exciting theatrical experience. Yet it will surely be agreed that the most permanently satisfying experiences are those which result from a harmonious collaboration between actors and producer to incarnate the intentions of the author. One of the differences between a drama school and a university drama department is that to the latter the play is of prime importance, actors and producers being viewed as interpreters – Chekhov is more important than Stanislavsky; Shakespeare than Garrick; and Molière is more important as the author of *Le Misanthrope* than as the actor who first played the part.

If, then, it is agreed that the play itself is the most important of three necessary things, the ability to read a play with real understanding of both its meaning and its theatrical potential is required. It is an ability that can, to some extent, be taught, just as one can be trained to read a musical score. But one will not get very proficient unless one has enough acting ability to realize how the parts ought to be played, and this requires both knowledge and breadth of taste.

Though the distinction between good theatre and good drama is a false one, there are some plays which read well and act badly. This may be due to faults of construction or weakness of characterization, which in the study may be less apparent than the beauty of the poetry. But too often readers condemn plays because they fail to fit their preconceived ideas. Aristophanes cannot be dismissed because his comedies are unlike those of Menander; Shakespeare should not be used as a stick with which to beat Jonson; Wycherley was not trying to do the same thing as Molière, though he adapted two of his plots; and it is absurd to complain that *The Importance of Being Earnest* is less earnest than *A Doll's House*. This is obvious enough, but it is surprising how often responsible critics fall into this trap. During the last few years there have been books written to prove that Shakespeare's plays are more profound than Marlowe's, and that Webster and Middleton are not as good as Shakespeare. This is true, of course, but it does not help us to appreciate the diverse excellencies of Jonson and Middleton.

It is necessary to know something about the stage for which plays were orignally written, even if they can be adapted for different stages. We need to know that Athenian drama originated in the chorus, that it was performed in the open air in amphitheatres, that the actors wore masks, and that the stories dramatized were all well known. Above all, we need to know that tragedies were performed as part of a religious festival. Some of these characteristics are to be found elsewhere: masks were used in the *nō* plays of Japan; the chorus was used in Racine's *Athalie*, in some of Yeats' plays, and in Eliot's *Murder in the Cathedral* and *The Family Reunion*; mediaeval mystery plays used familiar biblical stories. But none of these has any great resemblance to Greek drama.

The difficulty of performing plays on a stage for which they were not designed was particularly apparent in adaptations of Shakespeare in the nineteenth century. The addition of scenery, footlights and a front curtain necessitated many cuts and some re-arrangement of the scenes. There is an equal difficulty in attempting to produce plays by Ibsen or Chekhov on a plat-form stage or in a theatre where the audience surround the stage, for both dramatists relied on realistic scenery.

*   *   *

Eric Bentley says that 'a born playwright is a man who does not need stage directions.' But most modern dramatists, follow-ing the example of Barrie and Shaw, who wanted their plays to be read as well as performed, provide elaborate stage direc-tions, descriptions of the settings, etc. At the beginning of *Man and Superman*, Shaw takes some 300 words to describe Roebuck Ramsden and his study; and his description of the setting of Act III, on the Sierra Nevada, is twice as long. With Shakespeare and his contemporaries it is quite different. Although editors have usually inserted indications of place – 'a room in the castle', 'another part of the forest', etc. – there is nothing of the kind in the original editions. Such indications are indeed misleading, for the Elizabethans had 'unlocalized' staging, that is to say, we are given indications in the dialogue of time and place only when it is necessary. Otherwise we are not expected to consider the place. In the third scene of *Othello*, for example, so long as the Duke is on the stage, we know that the stage represents a council chamber; as soon as he leaves the stage and Iago is left alone with Roderigo the place is no longer the same, even though the audience is not consciously aware of the change.

Sometimes, of course, Shakespeare emphasizes the setting.
We are continually reminded in the middle acts of *A Midsummer
Night's Dream* that the action is taking place in a wood at
night. The misty barren heath is vividly evoked in the first act
of *Macbeth*. In the first scene of *Hamlet*, we soon learn that
it is just after midnight ("'Tis now struck twelve'), that sentries
are on the battlements, that it is bitterly cold ("'Tis bitter cold
and I am sick at heart'), and that clouds are hurrying across the
face of the moon ('the glimpses of the moon'). Before the end
of the scene the cock crows and dawn breaks:

> the morn, in russet mantle clad,
> Walks o'er the dew on yon high eastward hill.

After he retired to Stratford, it has been suggested, Shakespeare inserted some necessary stage directions. For example,
after Volumnia has pleaded with Coriolanus to spare Rome,
the moment of decision is given in a stage direction: 'holds her
by the hand, silent'. We may suppose that there was a similar
pause in *Measure for Measure* before Isabella kneels to the
Duke to beg him to spare the life of Angelo. This pause was
inserted in Peter Brook's production of the play, but we can be
sure that he had rediscovered the intentions of the dramatist.

We can deduce a good deal about the way actors should play
their roles from the actual dialogue. In the closet scene of
Hamlet, for example, we are told about the behaviour of
Gertrude, Hamlet and the Ghost. Gertrude wrings her hands
after the killing of Polonius (35); Hamlet shouts at her (53);
on the appearance of the Ghost, amazement sits on Gertrude
(113); Hamlet's eyes are starting from his head (120) and his
hair is standing on end (123); the Ghost is pale and glares (126)
and he steals out of the door (134). In the last scene of *Othello*,
the doomed Desdemona gives a running commentary on the
Moor's expressions, necessary because they could not be
clearly seen by the audiences:

> And yet I fear you; for you're fatal then
> When your eyes roll so . . .
> Alas, why gnaw you so your nether lip?
> Some bloody passion shakes your very frame.
> These are portents; but yet I hope, I hope
> They do not point on me.

We can deduce the changing appearance of Macbeth from his wife's commentary:

> Your face, my Thane, is as a book where men
> May read strange matters . . .
>   Only look up clear;
> To alter favour ever is to fear.   (I.v)

>   Be not lost
> So poorly in your thoughts.   (II.ii)

> Gentle my lord, sleek o'er your rugged looks.   (II.ii)

>   O, these flaws and starts . . .
> Why do you make such faces?   (III.iv)

So, in the scene in England, we are told that Macduff, to conceal his grief, pulls his hat over his brows.

The comments on gesture and appearance scattered through the dialogue provide useful hints to the actor, but they are less important for the interpretation of the part than the information he can glean about more fundamental aspects. Modern playwrights will frequently give an elaborate description of a character on his first appearance. This can sometimes be constricting. It is lucky that we don't have the author's views on Lady Macbeth's physical characteristics. But even Shakespeare, or the editors of the First Folio in which many of his plays first appeared in print, makes it clear in the *dramatis personae* that Iago is a villain, Roderigo a gulled gentleman, Lucio (in *Measure for Measure*) a 'fantastic'; and we are told in the dialogue that Rosaline is a brunette, that Helena (in *A Midsummer Night's Dream*) is much taller than Hermia, and that Rosalind is uncommonly tall.

A favourite device of dramatists is to describe the appearance of a character before his entrance – the yellow stockings and cross-gartering of Malvolio, the appearance of Petruchio at his wedding with the Shrew, or Romeo's account of the apothecary. The delayed entrances of Celimène (in *Le Misanthrope*), of Tartuffe and of Congreve's Millamant are all prepared by previous conversations about them. Restoration playwrights sometimes gave a full-length sketch just before the entrance of a new character, so that we can observe them behaving in the way described. In the first act of *The Way of the World*, Fainall and Mirabell discuss Witwoud:

FAINALL: . . . he has something of good Nature, and does not always want Wit.

MIRABELL: Not always; but as often as his Memory fails him and his common place of Comparisons. He is a Fool with a good Memory, and some few Scraps of other Folks Wit. . . . He has indeed one good Quality, he is not Exceptious; for he so passionately affects the Reputation of understanding Raillery; that he will construe an Affront into a Jest; and call downright Rudeness and ill Language, Satyr and Fire.

FAINALL: If you have a mind to finish his Picture, you have an opportunity to do it at full length. Behold the Original.

Enter Witwoud.

Apart from what the author tells us directly, our idea of a character is derived from what he does, what he says, what other characters say about him. Each of these sources of information may be misleading in one way or another. In a farce, the actions of a character may tell us nothing about him: he acts as he does because the plot requires it. Then again, the motives for actions are more important than the actions themselves (except in existentialist plays where a man is defined entirely by what he does). We have to ask why Cleopatra commits suicide, why Iago plots against Othello.

What a man says can be straightforward or ironical, deceptive or self-deceptive, and even out of character. When Othello, after the murder of Desdemona, is asked what shall be said of him, and he replies

An honourable murderer, if you will –

we cannot be sure if this is irony or self-deception.

Many dramatists put comments on the action into the mouths of sympathetic characters, so as to guide the responses of the audience, as when Edgar comments on the mingling of sense and nonsense in Lear's ravings:

> O, matter and impertinency mixed!
> Reason in madness!

Sometimes, however, such choric comments may be put into the mouth of a very unexpected character. Bosola, the malcontent murderer in *The Duchess of Malfi*, disguised as an old man, prepares the Duchess for death in speeches which seem to express the views of the dramatist:

> Didst thou ever see a lark in a cage? Such is the soul in the body: this world is like her little turf of grass and the heaven o'er our heads, like her looking-glass, only gives us a miserable knowledge of the small compass of our prison. . . . Thou art some great woman, sure, for riot begins to sit on thy forehead (clad in grey hairs) twenty years sooner than on a merry milk-maid's. . . .

> Much you had of land and rent;
> Your length in clay's now competent:
> A long was disturb'd your mind;
> Here your perfect peace is sign'd.
> Of what is't fools make such vain keeping?
> Sin their conception, their birth weeping.
> Their life a general mist of error,
> Their death a hideous storm of terror.

It may be argued that in these speeches Bosola is playing a role and that, therefore, he may be permitted to express sentiments somewhat alien to his character. But in his own death speech, he speaks even more obviously for Webster:

> Oh, this gloomy world!
> In what a shadow, or deep pit of darkness,
> Doth, womanish and fearful, mankind live!
> Let worthy minds ne'er stagger in distrust
> To suffer death or shame for what is just.
> Mine is another voyage.

The confession, in the last four words, that Bosola's mind is not worthy may be an attempt to make the speaker resume his character; but it is possible to defend the consistency of Bosola's utterances by the theory that despite his actions he admires virtue even in his victims and that his own conscience is never entirely deadened.

There is, indeed, some drama which is concerned not with human beings but with abstractions. The English morality plays contain figures which represent virtues and vices. *Everyman*, for example, has one central character, a generalized portrait of humanity, and such symbolic figures as Good Deeds, Fellowship and Five Wits. The religious *autos* of Calderón are similar in content. Paradoxically, some of the symbolic figures have human characteristics, and it has even been argued that in *Everyman* and other morality plays there was an advance in characterization.

*   *   *

The prose dialogue of some plays appears to be almost a transcript of actual conversation, though every dramatist refines and selects even when he is endeavouring to be as naturalistic as possible. Congreve, in the epistle dedicatory to *The Way of the World*, claimed that its polished style was the result of his acquaintance with Lord Montague; but, of course, no people in real life have ever talked as brilliantly as some of Congreve's characters. It has been pointed out that Shakespeare's prose dialogue, which seems perfectly colloquial, is further away from the actual speech of the period than that of Middleton, Dekker and Jonson.

Verse drama is inevitably less naturalistic, though T. S. Eliot, in his later plays, experimented in a verse form which, he hoped, his audience would not recognize as verse. The Elizabethans wisely alternated verse and prose according to the nature of the scene: comic characters, madmen, servants, etc., usually speak in prose; the upper classes usually speak in verse. There are many exceptions, however, notably in the plays written by Shakespeare in the last few years of the sixteenth century: Beatrice and Benedick, Shylock, Rosalind and Orlando, Falstaff and Prince Hal speak mainly in prose.

It is easier to differentiate one character from another by their mode of speech in prose than in verse. It is particularly difficult in the rhymed alexandrines of Corneille and Racine and in the heroic couplets of Dryden's plays, where the characters seem to declaim to one another in an identical style. It is much easier in blank verse. One has only to think of the varying styles of Hamlet, Claudius and Polonius, or of Othello, Iago and Desdemona to realize that Shakespeare gives each of his main characters a different style. It has been pointed out, for example, that whereas Othello and Iago both use many images from seafaring, Iago's are technical and pedestrian, Othello's 'romantic' and poetic; and that though both men refer frequently to unpleasant animals, reptiles and insects, Othello only does so after Iago has infected him with jealousy.

Not merely is imagery used to differentiate character; it can create atmosphere; and it often reflects the main themes of the play. A more subtle use is not so frequently noticed. It can, at times, express the unconscious mind of the speaker in opposition to the arguments he is using. The most famous example is Macbeth's soliloquy in I.vii. In it he argues that, although he would risk going to hell, it would be unwise to kill the King, partly because he fears that his death will be avenged and partly because Duncan is such a good king that his murder would shock people. But from the imagery of the same speech we are made aware that it is not only prudential motives that deter Macbeth, but a genuine moral repugnance:

> His virtues
> Will plead like angels, trumpet-tongued against
> The deep damnation of his taking-off;
> And pity, like a naked new-born babe
> Striding the blast, or heaven's cherubin horsed
> Upon the sightless couriers of the air,
> Shall blow the horrid deed in every eye
> That tears shall drown the wind.

Macbeth's style is quite different from that of his wife. She tends to use simpler, more prosaic language – except in her invocation of the evil spirits – and she is fond of using proverbial expressions:

> To alter favour ever is to fear ...
>   'Tis the eye of childhood
> That fears a painted devil ...
> Letting 'I dare not' wait upon 'I would',
> Like the poor cat i' the adage.

In the sleep-walking scene, she reverts almost to the monosyllabic speech of the nursery:

> What need we fear who knows it, when none can call our power to account? . . . Yet who would have thought the old man to have had so much blood in him? The thane of Fife had a wife; where is she now? What, will these hands ne'er be clean? No more o' that, my lord, no more o' that: you mar all with this starting.

There are certain disadvantages in the methods of naturalism. In Van Druten's *There's Always Juliet*, the heroine quotes from *Romeo and Juliet* to justify falling in love at first sight, and the poetry shows up the banality of the surrounding dialogue. If one compares a later scene, when the lovers part, with the corresponding separation of Romeo and Juliet or that of Troilus and Cressida, one can see that the language of poetry, though further away from natural speech, is more dramatic than Van Druten's prose:

LEONORA: I suppose we've got to say good-bye.
DWIGHT: Now?
LEONORA: I should think we might as well. It isn't going to get any easier. I'd come and watch you pack, put you on the train, only it would be just hurting myself. I'd rather get it over.
DWIGHT: O.K.
LEONORA: What were you going to say just then?
DWIGHT: Nothing.
LEONORA: What was it?
DWIGHT: It doesn't matter now. (*He holds out his hand*) Good-bye, then, Steve. Good luck to you.
LEONORA: And you. (*She takes his hand*)

CRESSIDA: And is it true that I must go from Troy?
TROILUS: A hateful truth!
CRESSIDA: What, and from Troilus too?
TROILUS: From Troy and Troilus.
CRESSIDA: Is't possible?

TROILUS: And suddenly, where injury of chance
Puts back leave-taking, justles roughly by
All time of pause, rudely beguiles our lips
Of all rejoindure, forcibly prevents
Our locked embrasures, strangles our dear vows
Even in the birth of our own labouring breath.
We two, that with so many thousand sighs
Did buy each other, must poorly sell ourselves
With the rude brevity and discharge of one.
Injurious time, now with a robber's haste
Crams his rich thievery up, he knows not how.
As many farewells as be stars in heaven,
With distinct breath and consigned kisses to them,
He fumbles up into a loose adieu,
And scants us with a single famished kiss,
Distasted with the salt of broken tears.

No one during a performance is likely to regard this passage as
at all unnatural. It expresses the pangs of parting more fully,
and much more intensely, than the Van Druten dialogue. It is,
of course, easier to give the illusion of naturalness in blank
verse than in rhymed couplets, at least to English ears. When
two pastoral lovers in Dryden's *Marriage à la Mode* describe
how they fell in love, they exchange some very pretty verses;
but we are more conscious of the charm of the poetry than we
are of the reality of the characters, especially as this scene
follows one written in modish prose:

LEONIDAS: When love did of my heart possession take,
I was so young, my soul was scarce awake:
I cannot tell when first I thought you fair;
But sucked in love, insensibly as air.
PALMYRA: I know too well when first my love began,
When at our wake you for the chaplet ran:
Then I was made the lady of the May,
And, with the garland, at the goal did stay:
Still, as you ran, I kept you full in view;
I hoped, and wished, and ran, methought, for you.
As you came near, I hastily did rise,
And stretched my arm outright, that held the prize.

> The custom was to kiss whom I should crown;
> You kneeled, and in my lap your head laid down:
> I blushed, and blushed, and did the kiss delay;
> At last my subjects forced me to obey:
> But, when I gave the crown, and then the kiss,
> I scarce had breath to say, Take that, – and this.
> LEONIDAS: I felt, the while, a pleasing kind of smart;
> That kiss went, tingling, to my very heart.
> When it was gone, the sense of it did stay;
> The sweetness clinged upon my lips all day,
> Like drops of honey, loth to fall away.

One can understand why T. S. Eliot preferred his audiences not to recognize that his plays were in verse. Yet it is quite possible to enjoy the poetry and at the same time believe in the reality of the situation and the characters. An extreme case is afforded by Kyd's *The Spanish Tragedy*, the most popular of pre-Shakespearian plays. Its popularity was partly due to its exciting plot, but also to the easily parodied, patterned speech:

> O eyes, no eyes, but fountains fraught with tears;
> O life, no life, but lively form of death;
> O world, no world, but mass of public wrongs,
> Confused and filled with murder and misdeeds!

It is worth noting that Ibsen, whose prose plays of modern life seemed to be so much more naturalistic than their predecessors, always insisted that he was a poet. As early as 1851, he asserted that 'in the realms of art pure reality has no place but, on the contrary, illusion'. Even after he began to write apparently naturalistic prose, he was aware of the element of artifice.

* * *

A frequent cause of imperfect sympathies is the critic's being used to a different kind of dramatic structure. The Englishman, nurtured on Shakespeare, tends to regard the closely knit structure of one of Racine's tragedies as too artificial; and the Frenchman, nurtured on Racine, could not but regard the looser structure of *King Lear* as inferior, if not barbarous.

There are many different kinds of plot. The simplest kind is a sequence of events in chronological order, which may be spread over a number of years. This kind, prevalent in the early years of Elizabethan drama, was mocked at by Sir Philip Sidney, in his *Apology for Poetry*, for showing the birth and marriage of characters in a single play. At the other extreme is a play such as Corneille's *Le Cid*, in which two fathers quarrel and one son kills the other father in a duel, has two agonizing interviews with the daughter of the man he has killed, wins a battle and fights another duel – all this in less than twenty-four hours. Don Rodrigue, the hero, has to keep one eye on the clock.

In another kind of plot, we are presented with only the last few hours in a chain of events which may go back for twenty years. Aristotle admired particularly the plot of Sophocles' *King Oedipus*. The story is virtually over before the play begins. Years before, Oedipus' father and mother, warned by an oracle that Oedipus would kill his father and marry his mother, ordered that the infant should be exposed. He is rescued and brought up as the son of the King of Corinth. When he reaches manhood, he is warned by a second oracle that he will kill his father and marry his mother. He flees in horror from Corinth and on the way to Thebes he kills his unknown father during a quarrel. On arriving at Thebes he solves the riddle of the Sphinx and is rewarded with the hand of Jocasta, his mother. Years later, after his children by Jocasta have grown up, Thebes is smitten with a plague. This is the beginning of the actual play, and all that happens thereafter is that the truth is brought to light, Jocasta commits suicide and Oedipus puts out his eyes.

Oedipus finds out the truth about himself, but the discovery is not a surprise to the audience, for they know (as did Sophocles' original audience) the outlines of the story before the play begins. The interest does not depend, as it does in a detective story, on surprise, but on the working out of the inevitable, on the inherent irony of the situation and on the ingenious economy with which the plot is contrived. In Cocteau's Oedipus play, *The Infernal Machine*, the action covers sixteen years, from the riddle of the Sphinx to the final revelation of Oedipus' birth.

If one considers two of Shakespeare's last plays, one can see the two methods of dramaturgy. In *The Winter's Tale*, the action covers sixteen years. The jealousy of Leontes leads to the

E

apparent death of his wife, Hermione, his estrangement from Polixenes, whom he suspected of adultery, and the loss of his babe, Perdita. After a lapse of sixteen years, the son of Polixenes is old enough to marry Perdita, and their marriage cements the reconciliation of Leontes and Hermione. The two halves of the play are linked by the oracle which hints that Leontes will find an heir and by a speech of Time.

In the next play, *The Tempest*, the action corresponds exactly to the time taken to perform it, from the shipwreck to the forgiveness of his enemies by Prospero. The initial crime – the deposition and exile of Prospero – had taken place twelve years previously; and the main action with which the play is concerned is – in addition to his forgiveness of Alonso, Sebastian and Antonio – Prospero's marriage of his daughter to the son of one of his enemies, his renouncement of magic, and his departure from the island. But the two underplots – the attempt of Sebastian and Antonio to kill Alonso and the attempt of Caliban and his associates to kill Prospero – are grotesque parallels to the conspiracy twelve years before. Shakespeare, had he so wished, could have followed the structure of *The Winter's Tale*, with a twelve-year gap in the middle of the play; but he chose instead to follow the more classical method of recounting past events rather than of presenting them on the stage.

Some dramatists succeed in revealing the past at the same time as they present an exciting action in the present. In Ibsen's *Ghosts*, for example, a great deal happens – Oswald's desire for Regina, the revelation that they are brother and sister, the burning down of the orphanage, the blackmailing of Pastor Manders, the collapse of Oswald, and the question left at the final curtain whether Mrs Alving will kill her son. But these events are subordinated to a gradual revelation of the past, in particular the relationship between Mrs Alving and her late husband. The pretence that he was noble is followed by the admission that he was a profligate riddled with disease; and this in turn is followed by Mrs Alving's admission that, as she never loved her husband, she was partly responsible for driving him to seek sexual satisfaction elsewhere. In *Rosmersholm*, by the same dramatist, there is a similar double action – or perhaps one should say a triple action. Kroll is seeking to prove that

Mrs Rosmer was driven to commit suicide, so that Rosmer will return to the religion and politics of his fathers; Rebecca makes two confessions, in the first admitting that she drove Mrs Rosmer to commit suicide, so that Rosmer would be freed to take an active part in radical politics, and in the second explaining that she was seized with 'a wild, uncontrollable passion' for Rosmer, though after the murder this turned into a calm love; and, thirdly, we watch in the course of the play the development of the relationship between Rebecca and Rosmer, ending with their suicide.

In some plays the plot is like a geometrical figure. In Racine's *Andromache*, for example, Orestes loves Hermione who loves Pyrrhus who loves Andromache, who loves the dead Hector. From this polygon of frustration emerges the tragic conclusion: Hermione commits suicide after getting Orestes to murder Pyrrhus; Orestes goes mad; and Andromache is left mourning her dead husband.

In some Japanese *nō* plays, the action is already over, but ghosts re-enact it. Yeats aimed at a similar distancing in some of his later plays. In *The Words on the Window Pane*, for example, the spirits of Swift and of the two women he loved, Stella and Vanessa, speak through a twentieth-century medium.

Most Elizabethan plays have one or more underplots. Sometimes these merely provide comic relief or have little connection with the main plot, but in the best plays they are ingeniously linked, structurally or thematically, with the main plot. In *A Midsummer Night's Dream*, for example, the framework is provided by the wedding festivities of Theseus and Hippolyta. Within this framework we have a quartet of lovers whose immaturity provides a contrast which is underlined by the antics of Puck. The irrationality of love is likewise shown in Titania's passion for the metamorphosed Bottom – beauty and the beast – and in the play performed before Theseus by Bottom's company. In *Hamlet* we are shown four avengers – Hamlet himself, Laertes, Fortinbras and Pyrrhus. Hamlet, the avenger of one plot, kills Polonius and so becomes the object of Laertes' vengeance; and the two men, in their different ways, love Ophelia. The plots of *King Lear* are likewise parallel. In both, a father is succoured by the child he has wronged, after he has been treated badly by the favoured children or child; the

evil daughters of one plot fall in love with the evil son of the
other plot; and he causes the good daughter to be murdered.
A third example, *The Widow's Tears* of George Chapman, has
two plots which are linked both thematically and structurally.
Both are concerned with the frailty of widows. The brother of
one 'widow' woos and weds the other; and this so shocks the
husband of the first that he tests his wife's promise never to
marry again by spreading a story of his own death and return-
ing in disguise.

*   *   *

The term 'comedy', as we have seen, covers a wide variety of
plays from Aristophanes' to Pinter's. Some comedies are just
love stories ending in marriage after misunderstandings or
trials of various kinds. Others depict characters behaving in a
ridiculous fashion, so that the audience laugh at them for not
conforming to the ways of society. Others, again, are used to
criticize not the outsider but the manners, or morals, or structure of society. It is possible to have a good comedy without a
single laugh, and even for it to come close to the edge of
tragedy. On the other hand, farcical comedy may keep an
audience roaring with laughter at the absurdity of situations
without throwing any light on human nature since the characters are mere puppets. Many comedies are a blend of more than
one kind. Even the most romantic comedies usually have an
element of satire; even the most satirical comedies often have
a love interest; and comedies designed to satirize the outsider
sometimes criticize the standards by which he is judged.

A few examples will illustrate these remarks. Aristophanes'
Lysistrata was written during the Peloponnesian War between
Athens and Sparta, and its didactic purpose was to persuade
the Athenians that they ought to make peace. Desperately
serious in intention, it is at the same time extremely funny.
Both the Athenian and Spartan women refuse to sleep with
their husbands until they agree to a peace settlement. The
possibilities of this situation are exploited to the full. Greek
drama, both comedy and tragedy, developed from the chorus;
and the two choruses in *Lysistrata*, male and female, give the
play some slight resemblance to musical comedy.

Twelfth Night, the quintessence of Shakespearian comedy, seems at first sight to be pure entertainment with no didactic purpose. Orsino loves Olivia who loves Cesario who loves Orsino. But Cesario is a girl, so that with the arrival of her twin brother the play can end with two happy marriages. The underplot, concerning the gulling of Malvolio by Sir Toby Belch and Maria, may appear to satirize puritan kill-joys and people who presume to rise above their station, though some sympathy is aroused for Malvolio at the end of the play and though Sir Toby's habits and his cheating of Sir Andrew make him a less admirable citizen than the ill-used Malvolio. But the Saturnalian spirit of comedy naturally prefers cakes and ale to loveless sobriety. *Twelfth Night* is not directly didactic, but Shakespeare makes us laugh at various kinds of sentimentality. Malvolio is 'sick of self-love' and hopes to marry Olivia only for this reason; Olivia is grieving affectedly for her dead brother; Orsino is not so much in love with Olivia as with the idea of love. The mockery, except in the case of Malvolio, is so gently administered that we do not realize at first that we are made to laugh at ourselves as well as at the characters on the stage. This process is assisted by the effect of the poetry of the dialogue and the music of the songs.

Ben Jonson's *Volpone*, written a few years after *Twelfth Night*, is a complete contrast. It is a bitter satire on avarice, to which sin nearly the whole of Venetian society is shown to be prone. Volpone himself, who worships gold instead of God, is a clever rogue: his victims are as evil, but they are foolish. Even the judges are corrupt. Although his scoundrels are all Italian, Jonson obviously intended his audience to apply the moral nearer home. But there is always the danger that this kind of didactic play, brilliant as it is, will leave the withers of the spectators unwrung and even make them congratulate themselves on being more virtuous than the characters depicted on the stage.

The next example, Molière's *Le Misanthrope*, is one of the masterpieces of the French theatre. The hero, Alceste, is priggish, self-righteous and humourless, and unable to make the compromises demanded by society. Molière shows him making enemies by his frankness, losing a lawsuit by relying on the justice of his case, and in love with a coquette. Alceste is held up as an absurd character who deserves to be laughed at; but Molière makes us see also that his hero's criticisms of society are largely valid. Some of Molière's plays are in prose, but this one, like *Tartuffe*, is in rhymed alexandrines which are both elegant and unobtrusive. The plot is of little importance: Alceste loses his lawsuit and sees through Célimène. The play therefore lacks the ingenious intrigue and bitter satire of *Volpone* or the variety and poetic beauty of *Twelfth Night*. What it does give is a series of brilliant scenes (e.g. the witty encounter of Célimène with the prude, Arsinoé; the quarrel between Alceste and Célimène; and the reading of Célimène's letters in the last scene of the play) which reveal the manners of society.

Congreve's masterpiece, *The Way of the World*, is also a comedy of manners; but so to describe it limits its significance. It is concerned rather with the conflict between the manners of the age and genuine feeling. Millamant has to pretend that she is like Célimène, although in fact she loves Mirabel violently. To speak of it as a comedy of manners tends to make one neglect Mirabel's struggle to safeguard the dowries of Mrs Fainall and Millamant; and it implies artificiality, though it is a realistic play and is artificial only in the continuous brilliance of the dialogue. No dramatist has written more effective dramatic prose and no one has so successfully used it to differentiate one character from another. Its one weakness – if we may judge from a frequently voiced complaint – is that the plot is difficult to follow at a first hearing.

Bernard Shaw does not satirize individuals for being aberrations from the normal standards of society: he satirizes society itself by the standards of an ideal. In some of his plays one of the characters acts as Shaw's mouthpiece, although both Tanner in *Man and Superman* and Shotover in *Heartbreak House* are also deflated at times. Sometimes, however, the message of the play is expressed by no one character: it emerges from the clash of opinions. In *Major Barbara*, for example, it cannot really be said that Barbara's Christianity, Cusin's socialism or Undershaft's religion of power can be equated with Shaw's own views. Undershaft acts as the tempter of the other two principal characters, forcing them to face the problem of power. They emerge from their ordeal with their faiths strengthened by their having shed their illusions. Although Shaw's plays generally contain discussions, in which the debaters are all gifted with eloquence, he makes use of a variety of theatrical forms, burlesque, melodrama, costume drama, fantasy, which he alters to suit his purposes. In some of his late plays he even seems to be influenced by the example of Aristophanes. He claimed himself that his models were Shakespeare, Mozart and Verdi: by which he meant that his plays should not be taken as slices of realism but that he was using some of the licence of a poet. The long rhetorical speeches put into the mouths of his characters have often been compared to operatic arias.

When we turn to Chekhov, we find that his idea of comedy is unlike that of any previous dramatist. Even *The Seagull*, in which the nominal hero commits suicide and the heroine, deserted by her lover, fails as an actress, is called a comedy by Chekhov, by which he meant, presumably, a balanced picture of life. In *The Cherry Orchard*, one of his greatest plays, there is a mingling of laughter and pathos. Looked at from one angle, Madame Ranyevskaia, whose son has been drowned, whose lover has treated her atrociously, and who is compelled to sell her beloved orchard, is almost a tragic figure. But in her fecklessness and her inability to face reality she is also comic. The scene near the end in which Lopahin is left to propose to Varia, Madame Ranyevskaia's adopted daughter, is funny and pathetic at the same time. The play, like most of Chekhov's, could be taken as a portrait of a dying class; but the characters are presented objectively, not held up to our mockery.

Tragedies are equally varied in kind. Not only does Greek tragedy differ radically from that of the Elizabethan age, that of the age of Louis XIV and that of Ibsen and O'Neill, but the tragedies of Aeschylus differ from those of Sophocles, and those of Sophocles from those of Euripides. It has even been said that there is no such thing as Shakespearian tragedy, since each tragedy differs from all the others.

The tragic hero can be almost wholly evil (e.g. Richard III) or almost entirely good (e.g. Ibsen's Rosmer, Sophocles' Antigone), a great man flawed (Othello) or a very ordinary man (as in Miller's *Death of a Salesman*). He can be destroyed by the operations of fate alone, or by a villain, or by some weakness of character, or by a combination of all three. Macbeth, for example, is brought to his ruin partly by external evil (in the guise of his wife and the witches) and partly by his ambition. Tragedy is sometimes caused by a conflict of principles. In *Antigone* the heroine's determination to give her brother a decent burial conflicts with Creon's command: both act according to their consciences. In the same way Shaw's St Joan is guided by the inner light, but the church which condemns her is not depicted as evil. In some tragedy there is a conflict between man and society; in some the conflict is in the mind of the hero. In existentialist tragedy a man is defined by what he does: the hero is entirely responsible for his own fate.

In recent years the most characteristic genre is neither tragedy nor comedy, but an interfusion of the two. This is not usually the tragi-comedy of previous epochs, in which a serious action is brought to an unexpectedly happy conclusion; nor is it tragedy with comic relief. It is more often 'black' comedy, in which the laughter aroused is uneasy and in which there is an undertone of horror or nihilism.

*　　*　　*

For the sake of clarity we have attempted to isolate some of the qualities that go to make up a good play, and these can be analysed by the reader. But it is important to realize that in the theatre we experience a play quite differently. If the production is a good one, the spectator will hardly be aware of the structure of the play, of the element of artificiality in the dialogue, of the creation of atmosphere by means of poetic imagery or even of the way the dramatist has created apparently life-like or symbolic characters, though these things will doubtless register on his unconscious mind. A good producer will be very much aware of all these things, and he will use both the personalities and talents of his actors and, where appropriate, lighting, scenery and costume to provide an experience of which a reading is only a shadow. Although, as we have argued, the script of the play is of prime importance, it exists fully only in performance. Nor is there a single right way of producing a masterpiece. Each one will vary according to the interpretation of the producer and the talents of his actors.

3

Acting

John Fernald

'Communication is the most important thing in life: it is what makes the human predicament bearable. And art is the most profound way in which one person communicates with another.' So once said Maria Callas, one of those opera singers who is also a fine actress. Her words are majestic in their simplicity: they also happen to tell us in two short sentences both what the actor does and the reason that he does it.

Acting is an activity which is as misrepresented and misunderstood as any that has occupied man throughout his entire history. Acting is not the 'pretending to be somebody else' that children find themselves doing from as far back as they can remember in the nursery. Neither is it the realizing of the fantasies with which adults compensate for a boring occupation or a dissatisfaction with their condition. Neither is it a therapy for people who suffer. Any or all of these considerations are dominant in 'acting' (I put the word between quotation marks to indicate that indulgence of dressing up and 'behaving' in public on the stage which is widespread in schools and amateur societies and which, though it has its place as an educational and social activity, has nothing to do with Acting). Acting, in its true professional sense, though it may partake a little of pretending, of realizing fantasy or of achieving a therapy, is a different matter. Acting is communication. It is difficult to define in its totality, but, if I had to define it, I would say that it is the discovery of a truth implicit in an author's words and the *communication* of that discovery to a live audience, some elements of which are a good deal further away from the actor than people normally are when they communicate with one another by unamplified speech.

The difficulty of Acting, as opposed to 'acting', lies in this duality. The actor has to be 'true'; but he also has to be the communicator of what is 'true'. To forget this duality is to admit the fog which for years has clouded much discussion of the subject: it is also to give cause to the multiplicity of half-baked theorizing which is substituted for hard work whenever two or three are gathered together in an American college theatre programme, or in that kind of amateur drama society which takes itself seriously and has no sense of proportion about itself. Historically, there seems always to have been some sort of dialectic between the truth of acting and the giving of that truth to the audience. Sometimes the emphasis has been laid on sincerity and honesty of interpretation; sometimes it has been on the technique of how an audience is actually 'hooked' by the actor's power. The facts of the matter are that the sincerity and the technique go together; the discovery of 'truth' goes hand in hand with the discovery of how this truth reaches the audience, undistorted and unweakened by the process of communication. Too often has it been supposed (Lee Strasburg and 'the method' are a case in point) that truth is one thing, while technique is something else – and something by which, more often than not, truth is falsified. To think this way is to fall into the trap of believing that, when he is acting, the expression of the truth will be guaranteed to the performer, provided his instinct for the truth is undeviatingly followed. The 'Method' actor has often been heard to say: 'If I *feel* it this way, it must be right.' That is not so. It doesn't matter what the actor 'feels'. What matters is what the audience 'feels'. The audience is the reason why the actor is there: he is there to give to an audience. Acting is the diametrical opposite of self-indulgent 'acting'.

But in giving to the audience there is also a trap, and it is because professional actors fell into this trap at the end of the nineteenth century that Stanislavsky felt impelled to explain what had gone wrong and what could be the means to put it right.

Before describing this trap more explicitly, the needs of the audience should be examined, and the reasons for their going to a dramatic entertainment in the first place should be understood. Historically, the Western theatre's roots lie deep in three sources: in the ceremonial enactment of religious myth by the Greeks, in the poets and tellers of stories (whose own roots go even deeper) and in a basic propensity of certain human beings for an irreverent and clownish exhibitionism which satisfies man's need for laughter. In these activities there are climaxes in which what happens reaches a moment of greatest fervour, or greatest excitement, or the extreme of absurdity. Men cannot, however, continue indefinitely at a high pitch of experience without the relief of an intervening 'low' in which to relax and return to normal; therefore, a pattern and a discipline appeared, as drama crystallized into becoming its recognizable self with the drama of Greece. The pattern consisted simply of the natural alternation between the 'exciting' and the 'not so exciting', with the audience's tension increasing as they participated in the former and relapsing into relaxation as they 'rested' during the latter. With the third root of modern theatre, with the clowns of Rome, growing into the Venetian comedians of the Commedia dell'Arte, and through the Elizabethans and their successors into the comedic acting that we know today, the same rule applied. It had to apply: man can only laugh for a certain length of time; the explosive violence of his reaction to what is funny has a limit to it, after which he needs a rest before he is physically able to laugh again. And so this ebb and flow of tension gradually gave form to drama. It has shaped all great drama since the Elizabethan age, and as theatre developed towards the complex discipline it became in the late nineteenth and early twentieth centuries, so the idea of emotional ebb and flow influenced the constructional technique of the playwright. Despite the apparent denial today of this form (the temporary going out of fashion of the 'well made' play), the form itself is what has shaped the art of the actor throughout history, and it is still influencing his way of acting today. (Although the novelty of some of the formless anarchic dramas of the moment do attract a section of the public, and therefore, of necessity, can attract the actor, who has his living to make, the 'rootlessness' of the anarchic drama does not satisfy most modern actors, because much of it takes from them the tools with which they work.)

Traditionally, the tools of the actor are appropriate to this alternate tension and relaxation which, despite anarchic drama, audiences still subconsciously need. Actors, by means of their technical training (a brief survey of which comes later in this chapter), hold a power over the audience. By this power they can not only indicate and emphasize these alternations, they can actually create tensions and relaxations of their own. They need to do this – through manipulating the tempo, pitch and volume of their speaking, through their use of pauses and through their control over facial and bodily expressiveness – so that the audience is never lulled by monotony into becoming apathetic. (Consider the reverse of this: the technique of a professional hypnotist. The hypnotist, who *wants* to put his subject to sleep, succeeds in doing so only by deliberate monotony in the pace and vocal line of his speaking.) So the audience's need for variety is, in fact, what places it within the actor's power – provided the actor has the technical means with which to exploit this need. Now it is easy to see where lies that second trap: if an actor has a power over the audience which is given him by his technique, it will be easy for him to misuse that technique and thereby use the power wrongly. His ability to control his audience is an aspect of his trade which he finds enjoyable. Unless he is gifted with judgment and good taste he can indulge himself and falsify the truth of his text. This is precisely what those tasteless, but technically efficient, nineteenth-century actors did in Russia, thus causing the Stanislavsky revolution to begin at the time of the discovery of Chekov's plays. (These, I think it is fair to say, would have forced the revolution even if there had been no Stanislavsky: the direct influence of Chekhov over performers was something which we should not underestimate.)

To sum up: acting, in this century, is an interpretive art which seeks the truth hidden in the writer's script, and which must then give this truth to the audience by means of technique; the technique is applied through a power over the audience which is due partly to the technique itself, and partly to the fact that the audience has to be enlivened by constant variety in the way the actor uses his tools; such power gives the actor an ability to cheat, through misusing it, so that if he is either tasteless or self-indulgent, he can distort truth instead of communicating it.

Thus, it is clear that the actor's responsibility is very great and is proportionate to his ability. He has a positive duty to communicate the truth of great writers (indeed of all writers whom he interprets). He can so easily do the very opposite. He must therefore be a man of dedication, an unselfish man. Yet because the theatre is a field where vulgarity can thrive as easily as good taste, where foolishness can be decked out to look like wisdom, where self-indulgence and desire for self-aggrandizement actually pay dividends, the temptation to be merely effective instead of true is strong. There is but one safeguard, and that is for the actor never to forget that it is authors, and not actors, that make theatre history. It is the authors who ultimately determine whether the theatre of a country is good or bad. The author must be put first at all times. His truth is there to be discovered, added to, indeed, by what perceptiveness and imagination is brought to it: it is never to be trifled with to satisfy the actor's vanity. Yet even as this is said, it has to be admitted that the very qualities that cause a person to want to be an actor – an aggressive ego and a dominating personality – are such as to make the preservation of integrity difficult.

Now let us attempt to go further towards the heart of the matter. Acting is giving. It is a service, ideally performed by a dedicated unselfish man, for the pleasure and satisfaction of the audience. It is, as Maria Callas has said, 'communication'. Let us examine how the actor communicates, and what training he requires in order to be able to do so. When this has been done, we can return to the question of what exactly is the truth communicated and how the actor finds it. It is important to realize here that success in the search for the latter is valueless unless the performer is able to use his tools properly: 'truth' which never reaches the audience might just as well have never been discovered.

Salvini, the great Italian actor, was given to making a simple statement about acting. It was also a very true one. 'Acting is voice,' he said. 'Voice, and more voice and again, more voice.' Without an effective vocal instrument the actor is useless;

however perceptive he may be about human psychology and human character, he lacks the means to convey his message. His voice, when trained, has to be able to be used in a number of ways. If playing King Lear, for example, he must be able to impress the audience by an enormous ability for sustained volume: if he cannot do that, then he cannot rise to the storm scene; the noise of the storm must then either drown his efforts entirely, or else it must be curbed and reduced to a few symbolic and not very loud flurries of wind and rain. That would be contrary to Shakespeare's intention: in the storm scene Shakespeare is pitting the elemental superpower of nature against a man who seems madly to be striving to be its equal. For the scene to reach the audience with its truth unimpaired, the largeness of scale must be preserved.

But mere capacity for volume is not by itself enough. The voice must be coloured by feeling: it must be capable, in fact, of conveying a great many kinds of feeling. Consider King Lear's range, from his almost supra-human defiance of the elements in 'Blow winds; and crack your cheeks! Rage! Blow!' to his heartbreak in 'Never, never, never, never, never!'

Consider, too, the extraordinary number of different *nuances* of thought and feeling which he expresses within that range in the course of the play. The voice which can convey the necessary power, variety and subtlety must, in fact, be a musical instrument which, if it were a man-made product, would be described as sophisticated and highly complex. Stanislavsky refers to 'a resonant form of speech which we note in great actors in moments of genuine inspiration'. He goes on to make this important point:

> An actor, interpreting a part in terms of his own understanding of it will not forget that each sound which forms a word, each vowel as well as each consonant, is a *separate note* which takes its place in the tonal chord of a word: it expresses this or that small part of the soul of the character that filters through the word.

The basis of the actor's vocal resources is the amount of breath with which he must fill his lungs. It is noticeable that the professional actor never appears actually to *take* a breath, only to *use* the breath he has. If an ordinary woman were merely to read Iris' speech in Shakespeare's *Tempest* (IV.i):

> Ceres, most bounteous lady, thy rich leas
> Of wheat, rye, barley, vetches, oats and pease. . . .

she would be likely to destroy the lyric flow of that poem by taking a breath in the wrong place. This would result in a jerky staccato delivery, instead of the smooth flow which the nature of the words demands. If an untrained actress were to attempt an emotional speech of a kind involving a torrent of words (St Joan's 'Light your fires', for example, in the trial scene), the sound of her intakes of breath in the wrong places would be noticeably gasping and unpleasing to the ear. (By breathing in the wrong way she would also strain her throat, and this would eventually lead to laryngitis.) So actors have to learn to give to their breathing certain capacities not possessed by non-actors: they must breathe so that they have wide ranges of volume and pitch as well as the ability to colour their tone with an infinite variety of emotional tints; furthermore, their lung capacity must be such that they can speak very long sentences in a single flowing phrase, while possessing a degree of breath control which enables them to take a breath when they wish to, never when they are forced to do it. And they have to use the voice in a way which does no damage to their health.

For Salvini a proper vocal technique was the vital quality to be expected of a good actor. His insistence on 'Voice, and more voice and again, more voice' was not simplistic. It is true that if an actor has great range and a complete vocal mastery, his excellence in that department can make up for defects in other aspects of his technique. The voice, after all, does most of the work of communicating with the audience. But it does not do all of it: movement, facial expression, the intelligence behind the eyes, to say nothing of the mysterious empathy created by the actor's intensity of imagination – all these are also means of communication.

Movement is an important means. A gesture, a turn of a head, sitting down, standing up, moving away a couple of paces – all these things can often take the place of the words which the author has written. The experienced author will usually welcome such a substitution, and the actor or the director may often suggest it. These people know that where a means other than words can achieve the same result, it is wise to 'change key', so to speak, to use the language of movement rather than the language of words. The audience, which always benefits from such variety, because it is stimulated by it, is provided with a new freshness of approach. The effect is exactly the same as that of the composer's key change trick: when he wishes to repeat a good tune a third time, the composer invariably changes the key signature, knowing that by this means he is insured against spoiling the effect of a good thing through over-doing it.

Discipline over the way an actor moves and makes his gestures is essential too. Amateur actors always move too often and generally make too many visual effects, and when they do so the result is distracting. The eyes of the audience will always be caught by a movement which they do not expect, and, as the eyes watch the distraction, the ears of the audience lose their hold on what the actor is actually saying (the reason being that no audience is capable of fully reacting to more than one theatrical effect at a time). So actors and director are always careful to *select* a visual effect and to use it where they think it will work best – in a place where it either emphasizes or does the work of a line which can then be cut. If they fail to select and to 'place' their movement in this way, the effectiveness of speech – which still does the bulk of the work of communication – will be blurred.

There are other ways in which the power to select becomes important. The timing of a line, or of a cross from right to left or of a glance can be a crucial matter. To wait two seconds may be wrong, while to wait three seconds may be right. In comedy acting, correct timing may make all the difference between a comedy effect working and getting its laugh and being an utter failure. (Comedy is the most scientific part of the art of acting: perfect accuracy in the use of its tools is essential.)

Before an actor can acquire the bodily control with which to put his effects where he wants them, and not where a nervous mannerism may force them on him, he has to learn how to relax. He has to learn how to relax, too, before he can achieve anything from his voice lessons. To use the body as an effective instrument of expression usually involves using one part of the body only – that part of it which is appropriate to the effect which the actor wants. The *rest* of the body must be in repose, otherwise it will distract by the kind of unconscious movement which the 'ordinary man' is always making. (How many times have we watched on television a politician or a bad actor banging a table or raising a hand at the wrong moment? He doesn't know he is doing it: he is unconsciously trying to emphasize his words with the additional support of movement; but the movement happens too often and in the wrong places, and the unfortunate fellow finds himself being rather less effective than he thought.)

The non-actor is unaware of this need for selection and has not learnt relaxation. Moreover, all civilized people have been conditioned by evolution to do things with their bodies that are not natural. To walk upright is an acquired ability; for our most ancient ancestors it was not 'natural'. To lead a sedentary life at a desk and to alternate that posture with the different posture needed to drive a car is not natural; we only believe it to be natural because we are now so accustomed to it. But we have only become accustomed to it through sacrificing the fully relaxed fluidity of body which we possessed in our primitive past. (A cat, for example, still has this fluidity.) In consequence we are subject to a great many muscular tensions of which we are hardly aware. The worst of these are tensions in the neck, in the lower jaw and in the shoulders. Such tensions get in the way of the relaxation required before a voice technique can even begin to be learnt. There are often tensions in the lips, which, when combined, as they frequently are, with 'lazy' tongue muscles, cause speech defects in the majority of the human race. Such defects may well be unnoticeable among ordinary people, who learn by habit and association to 'understand' words that are indistinct or mispronounced. But they are inappropriate to the actor, who has to speak with the utmost clarity if he is to communicate. Moreover, the actor sometimes needs to be able to speak not only clearly, but also extremely quickly; he therefore has to attain, through exercises, a positively acrobatic agility in the muscles concerned.

In the case of people who are not professional actors or singers, there is an important part of the human body – the

F

lungs – which doesn't even work properly. The lungs were once meant to be totally used, and so they were once fully operative. They should be able to expand and contract separately in different sections – bottom left, bottom right, top left, top right and, surprisingly, at the top back left and right just below the shoulder blades. But in the case of most of us, we breathe only shallowly, using nothing more than the top of each lung. Thus, most of us never breathe fully and can never get the capacity and reserve of breath we would need to take a long speech in our stride. An actor has to learn to develop his full, and not merely a sixth of his, lung capacity: shallow breathing leads to shouting and voice strain.

Relaxation is the key to discovery of all the things the body can do if the actor's discipline demands it. Relaxation is the starting point of every actor's training.

Such training, throughout most of the many centuries of acting history, did not exist in any organized way. Yet it is hard to believe that the most important basic principles of it were not handed down within the acting companies; certainly, experience must have taught the most talented actors how to make the best of themselves. By Shakespeare's day the emotional and psychological complexity of the long speeches in plays of the time must have given rise to a great deal of knowledge about speech and breath. (Interestingly, it is believed that Shakespeare's plays used once to be performed in fewer hours and minutes than they are today. This must have meant that the speeches were spoken far more quickly than actors speak them now – and this argues the existence of a certain degree of sophistication in the 'tricks of the trade' which were handed down, certainly as far as diction was concerned.)

Shakespeare's theatres were small, however, and so were the theatres of the late seventeenth and early eighteenth centuries. Theatres began to get big with the coming of artificial lighting, and with larger audiences the actors began to face the voice problems which they face in the modern theatre. The nineteenth century was notorious for its number of bad actors. The good actors were extremely few. They must have learnt by experience, by trial and error, to surmount the difficulties, and when they were the leaders of companies they were able to give the benefit, if they chose, to the apprentice actors round them.

In the nineteenth century voice teachers began to appear. It is probable that many of these were charlatans, for it is the easiest of fields for the quack, and, even today, first class voice teachers are not easy to find. (The voice charlatan is a dangerous fellow: a voice wrongly trained can be ruined for life.)

Today, training for the actor is accepted as necessary, just as it is necessary for the musician, the singer or the ballet dancer. The reason for the necessity should be obvious, since all performing artists do something which is in a sense 'super-human' and 'unnatural'. Any intelligent being can *imagine* that if he but had the necessary energy and brain to learn a trade or a craft, or to be expert in science or medicine or law, he could achieve the necessary result. But only an artist convinced that he has special gifts can *imagine* that he could ever seem to float on air like a ballet dancer or play a Paganini cadenza. It is the same with acting, yet the public attitude towards the actor's skill is not shaped by knowledge, simply because acting *looks* easy and 'acting' by amateurs is a common social activity. In fact, the easier skilled acting looks, the more difficult it actually is.

Good acting schools make Salvini's advice the basis for their training. Starting with showing each student how to find relaxation (a difficult thing in itself), they devote a great many hours to training the voice. This training, for which the 'ground rules' were laid down by Elsie Fogerty in the early decades of this century, is very meticulous. Elsie Fogerty founded the Central School of Speech and Drama, where she trained Sir Laurence Olivier. She also trained a number of first-class voice teachers, and so did her successor. All these teachers teach by the same method, as also do the teachers who learnt their technique at the Rose Bruford School in Sidcup, Kent. Uniformity of method is most necessary because the drudgery of continual voice exercises – comparable to the drudgery of a dancer's bar work – makes an acting student psychologically vulnerable. This drudgery is neither pleasant nor inspiring, yet the early stages are extremely important. If there is any doubt in a student's mind about the essential priorities in his early voice training, he quickly becomes insecure. Thus two voice teachers could both be 'right' and basically sound, yet a student being taught by first one and then the other could lose faith in both of them and in himself too–merely because of very slight differences of emphasis in the two ways of working. For this reason the Royal Academy of Dramatic Art was always careful to get its voice teachers from either the Central or the Bruford schools. These remain the best sources for really reliable voice teachers.

Next in importance to an actor's voice is his ability to move well. When the actor makes a movement in the middle of a speech he can make it either with or against the mood of the words – according to the context: either way he is bound to catch the attention of the audience in a most emphatic way. Consequently, unless his manner of moving is *appropriate* he can destroy his own effectiveness and, worse, that of the other actors. So he must learn to move expressively where the text demands it, and, equally, he must learn how not to move at all when the audience's attention is not supposed to be on him but elsewhere.

Movement should figure prominently in the time-table of any good acting school. But uniformity of teaching method, comparable to that in voice teaching, is not in practice attainable. Nor is it really desirable. There is a distinction to be made between the backgrounds of voice teachers and movement teachers. Voice teachers are not actors (though they have usually been trained at a school where they have acted with student actors). They are not performing artists, but have a vocational feeling about the instilling of vocal perfection in people who are, or are going to be, performers, and their satisfaction with life comes out of doing their work well and seeing their pupils succeed.

Movement teachers are somewhat different. Their backgrounds are nearly always that of ballet or modern dance, since there are no schools specializing in training people for the purpose of teaching movement for the theatre. Good movement teachers are more rare than good voice teachers. Dancers, unlike voice teachers, are artists by nature. They tend to find it unsatisfying to work with non-dancers and are often tempted to try to do more with them than is possible or wise (many a promising actor does not have it in him to be an outstanding mover: what is essential is that he should become an *acceptable* mover).

There have been choreographers and 'philosophers of the dance' who have sought to widen the scope of bodily expression and to extend it beyond the realm of dancing. Kurt Joos, with his ballet company, made his dancers almost into actors. Rudolph Laban evolved a language of movement which he claimed could even be used to enrich the lives of ordinary people. It is therefore natural enough that many movement teachers should have been trained by Joos or by Laban. Such training, however, is by no means an automatic testimonial of excellence. Too often has the possessor of an original mind tried to realize a vision, only for his disciples to turn it into a fad. The result of insisting that a young actor should obey to the letter the 'rules' which have stemmed from Laban's analysis of movement has more than once resulted in creating nothing but tension in the unfortunate pupil. Yet one of the best stage movement teachers I have known came from the Laban stable (as well as one of the least effective), and there are some ex-members of the Ballet Joos who have become brilliant teachers.

Uniformity of teaching – such as that necessary in the teaching of voice – is really only possible in the early stages of movement training. Here there is a common technique in dealing with such problems as bad posture and unrelaxed gestures and actions. Beyond this point the value of a movement class depends upon the imagination of the teacher rather than on his technique. It depends, too, on how much the teacher really wishes his talent to be of benefit to actors and the theatre. The actor learns best, I believe, from a teacher whose dancing experience has been in modern dance, not classical ballet (which tenses non-dancers who attempt even its most elementary postures). The most inspiring movement teachers in my experience have been those who made no attempt to expound a 'language' or 'philosophy' of movement, but have merely worked freely out of their own imaginations.

With voice, movement, and the timing of effects, we have described all those things which can be taught in a technical way: they are the grammar of acting, the 'how' of performance. We are left with the imaginative and creative part, and here the possibilities are infinite. There is no limit to imagination, there is no limit to discovery. In this field the verb 'to teach' must be clearly defined, since, strictly speaking, acting cannot be taught, and there should be nothing arbitrary about how an older actor suggests ways and means to a younger one. To say to an actor 'this is how you should do it' is to stifle completely his power to think for himself. The way, then, to 'teach' acting is for the instructor to give the student actor of his own experience, to show him instances of solutions to problems as the instructor once solved them for himself. Some of the solutions may settle the problems for one pupil; some may not. The best acting schools are those where solutions and ideas of all kinds are shot like arrows at the student from all directions: some will fall wide of the mark and others will stick, and what will work with one young actor will not necessarily work with another. But the profusion of related experience will stimulate the young actor and expand his knowledge of possibilities.

To think for himself as soon and as much as he can must always be the young actor's aim. If he falls short in this, he is in danger of becoming a purveyor of platitudes, using technical short cuts as substitutes for true creativity; he is also in danger of becoming 'director-bound', of becoming a mere puppet because he relies on the director for all that he does. Every actor must do his thinking in his own way; therefore, it can sometimes be of little help to him to learn how another actor does it. But an example of a particular way may serve to show how painstakingly thorough the process should be, and how deep it can go. What follows is an analysis of the creative process as one particular young professional saw it in her own case.

She began, of course, by reading the play, just as anybody else might have done. This gave her the general flavour, the 'feel' of the play that was to be her world for three hours on end eight times a week, perhaps for as long as six months of her life. Then she read it again, this time analysing it carefully and asking herself searching questions: What is the play really about? What is its period? What is its time span? What are the full circumstances in which each of the characters find themselves? Who *are* the characters? What are the relationships of them all with each other? Then she tried to look at each of the important characters, first from her own point of view and then from the point of view of the others.

The next step was to start thinking about her own character in detail and to find out everything about the part that she could possibly deduce from the information in the script: What was 'her' past life? How did 'she' relate to other people? What were 'her' mental and physical characteristics? What were the character's aims in life? An important element in this analysis was the comparison of any self-revelations made by the character with the statements about her made by other characters. If there was a difference between the two the actress immediately discovered something interesting and ambivalent about her part.

Then she delved more into the personality and basic motivations of the character. She had to think long and deeply about this, often finding the motivations so obvious that she overlooked them at first as mere clichés. When she had the full picture firmly in her mind she began *to imagine fully* the incidents she noted in the character's past life, writing down the facts in detail and then improvising – in her mind – exactly how they occurred. The italics are important: non-actors reading, let us say, a newspaper account of a family trapped in a burning house – seeing words describing first the children jumping from a high window into the shrubbery, some of them breaking limbs as they fall, and finally a frightened mother leaping out of a smoke-filled room with her baby in her arms, only to find that after the final escape into fresh air the baby is dead – *do not really imagine* the *reality* behind the journalism. They literally see *words*, and the words do duty for visions: very few people fully see the visions themselves. Visions, however, in all their detail, colour, and reality are what actors studying their parts have to see, with the perceptive eye of imagination. This takes a great deal of time and of concentration.

Now let us follow the working of our young professional in her successive steps. She begins to visualize her own scenes, keeping track of the effect, at the same time, of the scenes she is not in. She begins to visualize how the internal elements of the scenes – personality of the character, her conscious and unconscious motivations, would affect the external behaviour of *all* characters. She studies the dramatic shape of her scenes, finds the climaxes, seeks for the musical analogies which theatre always provides – the fast sections, the slower ones, the contrasts of pitch, tone, and volume. (These latter things are in the director's province, but she has not started rehearsing yet, and the more she brings to rehearsal – in her mind – the more the director will see her as good material from which to build his production. She will, of course, avoid making the director feel that she is anticipating his work or trying to influence it. She must be a good psychologist not only about characters in the play, but about everybody concerned in its presentation.) She needs finally to achieve a complete and familiar picture of all the circumstances, outer and inner, that affect her part so that, in imagination, she is fully able to 'live out' her character.

In much of this process she resorts to memories of her own past: remembering how she felt at certain emotional and climatic moments in her life. It is not necessary for her actually to have experienced what her part is supposed to have experienced: if as an actress she finds her baby dead in her arms, she does not need to have had such a tragedy happen to her. She will have known what it is like to love, and she will have known despair. Her 'emotion memory', as Stanislavsky called it, together with her powers of imagination, will give her the picture of the proper emotion that she will have to 'see'. Once she can bring into play a really vivid memory of a feeling towards a person, or a place, or an object, or once she can bring out of her memory an appropriate physical sensation, her imagination can then get to work to adjust these feelings so that they cease to be part of her private life and become fused with the character she is playing and also part of that character's relationship with others. Then it is up to a combination of the power of her feeling and the strength of her technique to make the audience 'see' what she sees.

All this work of discovery and association with memory has been going on for many days, possibly many weeks before the beginning of the rehearsal period. It continues when rehearsals start and as they progress. There comes a time when all the 'thinking' should stop and something yet to be described should be substituted for it: but this is not yet.

At rehearsal the actress will try as soon as possible to get familiar with the faces of the other actors and with their personalities. She will begin a process of seeing these faces and personalities not as 'actors', but as the 'people in the play'. She will try to imagine the physical surroundings of the play's action (she will have been shown a model of the setting or a picture of it, with reasonably accurate renderings of the shapes of furniture and scenic features), and her imagination will fill in these areas beyond the setting which the audience never sees. She will 'see' them, however, so that whenever she makes an entrance or an exit she will know exactly where she has 'come from', what she was 'doing', where she is 'going', and why. By trial and error, and through a good director's help, she will discover any physical eccentricities there may be about her character and how she should move and hold herself. She will find out in full detail what her character is doing, or thinking, or watching, at every single second of the progress of the scenes in which she appears.

Then there comes a time, somewhere about ten days before the first performance, when she must stop this process of deliberate and conscious discovery. It is extremely important that she should make this break with her previous method of working and that she should not make it too late. The best performers are those who know that in acting the thinking process must be disciplined and, at a certain point, actually banished. This allows a succession of quick intuitive reactions to build on top of the slow, laborious, 'intellectual' foundations. It permits the mystery of inspiration to be born. Dame Margot Fonteyn, as good an actress as she is a ballerina, once said that ideas came to her not through her brain, but 'through the pores of her skin'. There is a good deal of truth in this, but the more intelligent the actor the more difficult it is for him to convince himself that it makes sense. His undoing can come from his very cleverness, because, always critical of his achievements as rehearsals develop, he tries each day a new idea, while never perfecting and consolidating any of those ideas that came to him before. Thus he remains uncertain which of many ideas is best. He can only use one of them, and, when finally the curtain rises and he faces the audience, he plays that one. But it is unperfected, it does not have the player's conviction behind it, and it is likely to fail to impress as it should. (Many fully committed actors of modest talents can prove

better in performance than the 'brilliant' actors who are not
convinced that what they are doing is best.)

So, in the late stages of rehearsal our young actress has
settled for one particular way of working, one definite angle,
one solution to each of the problems of performance that she
has faced. Intuition has taken over, and with intuition has
grown ease and smoothness and an almost unconscious ability
(for her lines have now of course been thoroughly learnt) to
play the part.

She must now begin to imagine the coming presence of the
audience. She has always taken them very much into consideration in her thinking, but now, as the first performance approaches, she has to remind herself that the audience is the sole
reason for her existence, and that her job is to give all of her
craft for their benefit. Here the duality of theatre comes
again into her mind. She may have to adjust certain ways of
doing things simply in order that the audience may hear her
better or see her better: and in making the adjustment she must
insure that she never loses the truth of the part or of the play.

In performance she will continue to find out more about the
part, and about the play, and about herself as an actress. If the
play is a comedy, with plenty for the audience to laugh at, she
will learn how to 'get laughs' which at first she perhaps failed
to get. She will also find she can get laughs which perhaps her
taste, or her director or author tell her she ought not to get.
She must be on her guard lest, by giving the audience too much
of what they seem to want, she has been led to betray the true
quality of her material. If the play is an emotional one, there is
always a risk of over-acting, or of lengthening a pause which
was planned to express a thought or a feeling, to the point
where it has become too long and so slows up the performance
and bores the audience. (This is a common temptation: if a
pause seems 'good' because it rightly gauges time needed to
'feel fully', as well as time needed for the audience to react,
the actor can easily deceive himself that if the pause becomes
longer it will also become 'better'. But this is not so.)

There are other temptations. In acting one must never forget
that one is playing with other actors. One must look at them
when they expect it and make the right reaction when they
expect it. But when the extra relationship of actor-audience

develops, a performer can become so besotted with it (because he knows how to make the audience love him) that the other actors are forgotten.

Then, in an imperfect world, there may always be 'bad bits' of the play surviving into performance. These may be awkward sections of script not perfected by the author, not put right by the director, and possibly neglected, too, at rehearsal – only because they did not then seem all that bad and were perhaps linked to scenes which were seen to be very good. So these scenes in rehearsal were forgotten scenes. In performance those 'bad bits' are suddenly high-lighted for what they really are – sections of unreality, 'sore thumbs' which the audience reaction soon proves are not believable. Such imperfections have to be worked on and put right, not skated over.

Finally, of course, the performer must guard against tiring of the play or the part, should the run become a long one. Parts have to be re-thought, looked at again in all their dimensions, and sometimes it is a constant labour to keep their freshness alive.

To draw a conclusion from this chapter's statement: 'acting' may be 'fun', but Acting is hard work. It is, however, hard work which, if the talent and the sense of vocation is there, can bring an inspiring sense of purpose to the actor's life. No one should try to be a professional actor unless he is sure that he has talent, sure that he has the capacity of application, the patience to endure drudgery, and the courage to face failure – as well as the level-headedness to survive success with all its temptations. *No one should go on the stage at all unless he is unable to conceive of himself as being in any other kind of profession except acting.* He must accept that to act is to give, and that it is a privilege for him to be able to give to people an extended vision of life, a greater awareness of human relationships. He does this through a vision which a writer has seen first and which the actor, remaining faithful to the writer's intentions, has learnt how to make more clear. And he must see his job clearly, understanding that the *technique* of acting and the *imaginative processes* of acting are far from opposing ideas. They are each necessary and complementary aspects of one whole, as the Greeks knew when they made the word for *technique* and the word for *art* one and the same.

4

Production

Kenneth Parrott

In the case of some of the other chapters of this book, the titles are clear and readily understood. When one ponders the title of this section, however, a mass of complexities rush forward, in many cases overlapping with each other in terms of definitions and labels. What exactly do we mean by 'production'? The dictionary is almost flippant: 'total yield'. Clearly we must cover the waterfront. It does not matter too much in what order, but it might be worthwhile to sort out one or two possible misunderstandings as we begin.

The word 'producer' can conjure up either a cigar-chewing movie tycoon or the harrassed manipulator of the school play. It would be no use blaming either for muddling us: if they call themselves producers and everyone working with them does the same, who are we to challenge this? Happily words can still mean what we want them to mean. At the same time, in searching for definitions and descriptions of jobs, it will be helpful to have a look at current practice in the commercial theatre.

It is the nature of an image-conscious profession to become discontent with what may seem to be old-fashioned titles. 'Stage Manager' becomes 'Stage Director', soon to turn into 'Technical Director'; 'Manager' has to be 'General Manager', now 'Administrator'. More than presentation is involved, particularly when large organizations are considered. Very likely the status or definition of adjacent posts within the same company are as relevant as concern for semantic precision.

It will certainly not help clarify doubts by comparing titles or responsibilities with the practices of other media.

The titles of 'Producer' and 'Director' mean fundamentally different things in the theatre and in films and television. As the billing of the latter, often glamorous names is probably more familiar, let it be understood from the start that the theatre's use of 'Producer' and 'Director' must be considered quite separately. No useful purpose will be served by investigating television and film procedures here: let us merely accept that they can differ radically from those of the live theatre. In recent years the accepted practice has been for the title of *Producer* to be held by the impresario, or presenting manager, who sets up the whole production, while the man who takes immediate charge of the work of actors, dancers, designers, musicians and technicians is called *Director*. (The use of these titles varied somewhat until the early 1950s, but since then the current practice has been generally accepted in professional theatre in this country.) The definitions make clear sense in the commercial theatre. However rare, whatever its quality, the show is set up as a marketable product which exists only as long as it can be sold. It is therefore entirely logical for the man who 'makes' the product to be called the producer. It is important, however, not to proceed from this to assume that the producer's concern is merely financial and administrative while the director controls the rest.

The London producer's choice of the play may be based on sound judgment in reading scripts; it may also be the result of timely action in buying the play when seen in New York or in a provincial try-out. However chosen, the play will have small chance of interesting the essential investors without the guarantees implied by the contracting of some starry names in the cast and without the knowledge that the director has been associated with previous success. In some cases, the star actors are chosen before the director; in no case are plays cast by the director against the judgment of the producer. The designer may also be regarded as part of the sales promotion. This depends on the nature of the play. Naturally, the most satisfactory results come from respectful collaboration; but it would be idealistic to expect this to happen easily. The real truth of what takes place can only be known by the producers and directors themselves; much of what is reported, gossiped and publicized is less than clear. What is apparent and inescapable is the intertwining of artistic and financial considerations in setting up a production. Lavish commercial enterprises, budgeting in thousands of pounds, might seem an irrelevant area of comparison with modest amateur work. But, in fact, the pressure of financial circumstances can be just as strong, though the stakes are mercifully lower.

Let us take a simple hypothetical case: a well-organized amateur society is formulating plans for the forthcoming season and one of the members wishes to direct *Othello*. This choice of play is a marked contrast with the society's staple diet of recent West End successes with modern dress and yet another permutation of the stock, box-set flats for scenery. Let us assume that all is sweetness, and a likely cast is ready, willing and eager to go. Budget? Usually about £15 per production: in this case, a ridiculously inadequate figure. Costumes will cost about £65 to hire, and to make even a simple set from fresh materials will cost about £20. Then, some special lighting equipment, and a budget for music. . . . And the total creeps up to £150. But the society has never taken more than £75 on a successful run of four nights. Yet there are 100 seats in the hall, and if the production could play for six nights at capacity, at 25p per seat, then there would be no loss.

Nobody dares budget for capacity business except in very rare circumstances. Perhaps this is one of those rarities. The last Shakespeare done locally was years ago by an Arts Council touring group. Can we persuade schools to send parties, even if it is not a set text? Why not do it in modern dress and save the costume budget? How can you expect schools to support it if we do it in the 'wrong' period? Better to run for nine performances and make sure of good costumes. . . .

Complicate these and similar considerations (as they usually are), and very soon the luckless director wonders why he ever mentioned *Othello*. Does he abandon the project or accept the cut-down budgets and plough on doggedly hoping for something to work itself out? While he is wavering, the rights of *The Odd Couple* are unexpectedly released and that's the end of the play selection problem for that season.

Take a less despondent example: a year later *Othello* goes ahead. A kind benefactor has offered £75 towards the cost of the show, but with a proviso – instead of spending £65 on hiring costumes, the costumes should be made and kept as part of wardrobe stock for the benefit of future productions. The cost of materials is £30, the labour free. The same principle applies to the sets. Ingenuity saves 70 per cent of the earlier budget, and simpler more relevant ideas emerge. The cast strengthen their resolve to get the play on, to the extent of each offering a pound as a guarantee against loss. The gamble is taken and the production succeeds. Which were the artistic and which the financial decisions? Further, how was it that the right answers emerged?

Mercifully, our fictitious example has now evaporated, or we would be bogged down in its now unimportant details beyond the point of useful analogy. What remains clear in the memory is that *Othello* got produced, mainly because somebody wanted to do it and convinced enough other people to join him in presenting it.

Nobody can do theatre alone, and it does not matter who originally thinks of the idea. The essential next step is that, either by one man's persuasion or by the corporate concern of a group, the tasks that must be executed are apportioned and tackled towards the single aim.

Remove the commercial stimulus of making money, and a spectrum of motives can 'produce' theatre. There are few that succeed without handing over the project to a director. What is a director, and how do I become one? In answer to the latter question, Sir Tyrone Guthrie replied, 'When someone is mug enough to give you a stage to do it on.' To cope with the former question, we must first consider in details what happens when a show is prepared.

The decision to present a particular play in a certain place may very well not be the director's initially. This may be so in the case of an expensive commercial show as well as in the case of a modest amateur production. But once the decision to present a play has been made, the next urgent step must then be to fix a director. There are those who wish to argue from the hard grounds of commercial interest or the cosier concerns of 'group productions' that the director will become an overweening monster who needs putting and then keeping in his place. A director's insistence on the importance of sensitive casting can alienate him from the managerial right and the communal left. Whichever extreme is being followed, there will certainly come a time when a director has to be hired or consulted. The later the point in time that he is involved, the greater the risk of wasted time and abortive work. Whether we are concerned with a lavish production, dripping with all kinds of marketable commodities, such as glamorous leading ladies and star-spangled costumes and sets which hide almost everybody, or an avant-garde project which is crammed with subtlety, complexity and all the media ever mixed, it will become vital for one single judgment to select and arbitrate about what the audience must eventually face. Sooner or later, and far better sooner, an act of trust will be made in the choice of a director. His brief may well, incidentally, include making a management richer or a group or society more fulfilled. His rewards will be appropriately, and somewhat proportionately measured; but, in the senses that matter, his success or failure will reflect his skill and judgment in handling the people and the circumstances in which he does the job. From the director's point of view it might seem that the ideal situation would be for him to be rich and his theatre prosperous, thus making it a simple matter for the pure metal of his inspiration never to be reduced to the baser alloy of compromise. We may all dream, but this one is a long way from reality.

Like the resulting performance, the preparation of a production is a rich texture of the contributions of many people and situations. The prime duty of the director is to get good ideas flowing and to see how to blend them into the show. (Paddy Chayevsky once said, 'I don't care who has a good idea, as long as I get the credit.') Whether the director thought of the play first, or whether a manager or a company invited him to take over a going project, the essential condition of allowing him that charge is his desire to make it possible for everyone concerned to join the corporate, creative process that serious theatre demands. (Let us qualify two words in that sentence: 'desire' must be supported by skill and experience; 'serious' refers to the intention and application of preparation, rather than the chosen work. A thoroughly-prepared light comedy might well be 'serious' in the sense that an ill-organized and under-rehearsed classic tragedy could never be.)

'Interdependence in the theatre is complete. When it is not, something is functioning wrongly or not functioning at all.' Thus Harley Granville-Barker argued for 'an association of men and women co-operating in the practice of an art'. It is time for us to consider in more detail some of the prime functions and areas of skill involved in bringing a production to life. Various orders of priority could be suggested, and in most cases the selection would be arbitrary, depending upon the particular styles of production that were uppermost in the mind. Few lists, however, would not begin with the actors.

Casting, or the selection of actors and actresses to play the characters in the script, is a fascinating early stage in the preparation of any production. In respect of many plays and parts, the instinct for matching actor and character can contribute and stimulate in a way that no later action can. There is no pretending that for some plays, and a good many smaller parts, to cast as closely as possible to the actor's natural appearance will be the only satisfactory solution. If the figure of the ruthless soldier who suddenly enters to terrify a group of prisoners could offer no more than a skinny five-foot five in his thickest socks, it will take a good deal more than acting to make that moment 'work'. Nor would there be much pleasure or profit for all concerned in covering this kind of deficiency.

There is a pious axiom that there are no small parts, only small-part players. Whoever claims this should do penance in one of these parts until his judgment returns. By this time he will have gazed with envy upon the actors allotted parts with real substance and have noticed that in many cases the eventual performance belied first impressions on the first day's rehearsal.

If the director knows an actor and his work in thorough detail, intelligent casting will probably just happen intuitively. In this respect, a permanent company has a good chance of yielding perceptive casting, simply because of the daily opportunities for increasing awareness of skills and personalities. More difficult problems are posed when the director is considering actors whom he has either never met before or possibly

G

has only seen playing parts that are a long way removed from the style of the work in hand.

For many the routine process is audition; for most this method is disliked and mistrusted. Yet what alternative is there? Not to audition restricts the director to working with former colleagues and deprives the actor from introducing himself to new areas of employment or opportunity. An important contribution is made by *casting advisers*, who work in close touch with actors' agents. The casting expert can build upon a wide knowledge of the work and experience of the acting profession. Objectivity, combined with a nose for a developing talent, allows the theatre's equivalent of a marriage broker the chance to arrange a match between actor and character that may even surprise the director who sets the seal. If the audition is merely a recited set piece, all that can accurately be assessed are the sound of the voice and the shape of the body (and that can be disguised by choice of clothes). Some professional actors decline to offer themselves for this kind of audition, judging that the small amount of information it can impart can equally be revealed in conversation and that the nervous tension of offering an out-of-context snippet of a past performance gives an inaccurate impression of their true ability. Others bask in auditions like cats in the sun. The theatre is full of human beings with widely differing natures.

Some directors can elicit information (and discover aspects of an actor's personality) better from the distant darkness of the auditorium, while others thrive on close-range, private, almost secretive contact. One director will search for the actor's courage, identity and ability to entertain single-handed, while another will be more concerned with subtlety of response, and capacity for blending and being orchestrated into a general pattern. The same director may seek these different extremes for different characters in the same production, or dream of enjoying both in the same performer. He may take a chance on a brief conversation. He may well extend the audition into a more detailed 'work-out' in which special skills can be explored, tensions can be allowed to relax, so both actor and director may discover enough to know whether working together might succeed. Since so much will hang upon the sharing of trust, it is reasonable that the actor should have a chance to know something of his potential director. Reputation may do much, but several weeks' work at close quarters will follow acceptance. Failure may reward the actor financially just as much as success, but the misery and risk of damage to his future career could well off-set the material gain. Inter-dependence is a highly delicate reality in this work.

It would be impertinent to offer rules for casting: one might as well pretend to offer sure-fire ingredients for a perfect party. Since circumstances rarely offer a combination of all desirable characteristics in an available actor, 'successful' casting often results from close attention to less obvious personal traits and to relation to other actors engaged in the production. Physical appearance is clearly important: in many cases, however, it is easier to compensate for this than for more elusive qualities of an actor's or character's personality.

In any event, casting is undoubtedly an area in which the sole judgment of the director should be allowed to operate. A committee will never assemble a cast with the conviction that one instinct can achieve. To reduce the process to a short list and a vote will go the way of all examples of the highest common factor. In the theatre safety and the obvious usually tend towards mediocrity and boredom. If casting is persuaded into this direction, all the effort in the world will scarcely struggle to improve the situation. Some directors will argue that, once cast, any given actor no longer has a choice: the state of his development, the influence of his past work and the opportunities offered by the author all conspire towards a definable, predictable performance. To accept this as inevitable under-rates the roles of the director and fellow actors, to say nothing of any unexpected influence between the first rehearsal and the opening night.

Nevertheless, from the director's knowledge of the actor's capacity, much can certainly be predicted of his final contribu-tion. There is certainly no more influential decision than casting: it is both the earliest and the longest-lasting creative judgment that the director will pass upon each actor's work. Once again, the situation in a regular company is healthier than elsewhere. The director knows that he must cast from a given group of actors. Decisions are simplified, and all can come to terms with their commitments. In the wider-ranging commercial world, as long as there is another actor to interview, another suggestion to consider or one more day before the costume designer resigns, the director will be tempted to wonder, is he really right – could we not try ****? Are you sure ****'s film has not been postponed? Could you double-check ****'s television dates? I know **** will attract the backers, but we both know he will ruin the second act, because he could never look vulnerable in a thousand years, etc. Old or new, 80 per cent right or 60 per cent wrong, a decision will ultimately be taken and rehearsals can actually start.

While the casting has been going on, if we consider a production by a commercial management, an early investigation must be made of possible theatres in which to present the play. To any company which enjoys a permanent base theatre, to prepare a show for an unspecified stage may seem an act of folly. It frequently is – both unspecified and folly. The fortunes of West End productions can change so fast and involve such sums of money that theatres can become available at a week or two weeks' notice. New plays may flop almost on opening, while even a long-running production may drop unexpectedly below its minimum contracted revenue figures and the queue of some new shows will jostle and lurch as the next opportunist leaps into the vacant building.

As the size of theatres varies considerably, both in capacity and stage dimensions, a last-minute change in theatre may cause some hasty adjustments to have to be made to the set (already well advanced in construction, if not complete). Too large a stage may seriously diminish the effect of a small setting, while the opposite problem may leave significant parts of the acting area out of sight of much of the audience. The theatre is a resilient trade, and by the first night these difficulties will almost certainly have been dealt with. But the price of the adjustment may well be a vital aspect of the original intention or the fatigue and nervous strain of wrestling with the problem which will bear its mark upon the cast: 'If only we had known where we were going, to do it from the start. . . .' One of the most stimulating factors in design can be the relation between the play and the building in which it is to be performed. One says 'can be' because the practicalities of touring and West End management often make this impossible to plan. For this reason, productions often sit uneasily within unsympathetic structures, waiting for the house lights to pretend that the bricks and mortar are not really there.

When a company has a home base, a valuable tension can be struck between the theatre and the production. To achieve its maximum effect, the stage design must seem to 'embrace' the audience. This can be as true of proscenium staging as in any 'thrust' or 'arena' theatre. Assessing the total architectural context is a prime responsibility for the *Designer*. If the theatre were not also a commercial undertaking, this area could also be the concern of the creative impresario. A play that is right for the Criterion could hardly be good for the Adelphi Theatre. From the reverse direction, when work is being planned for a given theatre, the opportunities and limitations of the building can affect even the choice of plays as well as the style of the designs. At the same time, the designs must cope with the smallest details of nuance and practicality. It is no good achieving striking architecture and sensual excitement if the clothes are so cumbersome that fast, light movement is impossible. No effort, exercise or cajolery will circumvent the director's failure to warn the designer that Act 3, Scene 2, must be played on the run, employing staircases, swinging doors, flying crockery, chaos, and so forth, even if 'it is not usually done like that': this is a frivolous, fairly unlikely example, but let it be the token for a multitude of misunderstandings between 'direction' and 'design'. Both are part of the same process, in so far as the jobs are done by two people and communication between them is a fundamental need. Conflict, unresolved, will not only frustrate the director's intention, but it will also, very likely, place the actors in a trap or, at best, in situations in which they will have to waste precious time finding remedies.

We have assumed that one designer does everything 'seen'. In practice, the sub-division of set and costume design is frequent, if not the norm. From many points of view this is a pity, since it further fragments the 'view' of the production. Yet, if the director is right to delegate to a designer the look of the sets and if this designer has no real knowledge of how clothes are made, it is better that another should take charge of this job. Once again the importance of close communication cannot be too highly stressed. The actors must know what is planned: they will have to wear the costumes. The cast may not necessarily be right the first time about what to wear, but the spurious stimulus sometimes offered by providing a just-finished garment minutes before the final dress rehearsal will usually manage to make the costume wear the actor and the actor lose much life in the process.

Gradually, the modern theatre is becoming used to a few weeks' rehearsal without remorse or the blush of indulgence. The next battle to win is that sets and costumes should be ready during the early stages of work, part of the tools of the craft, made to be used by the craftsman. Last-minute surprise only makes the actor tend to ignore the designer's work. Details that have not been fully assimilated can scarcely be employed with conviction. This is as true of an ornamental jug as of an iron grille or a flowing train. Interdependence ... *should* be complete.

A fundamental part of the visualization of the play is, of course, the lighting. Ever since the theatre moved indoors there has been, at the very least, the requirement to illuminate the area of performance. At first, the area occupied by the audience was equally lit, but the advantages of emphasizing the acting area or leaving the audience in a dimmer light were natural developments, particularly when advance in techniques coincided with a growing concern for representing real life as accurately as possible. With present-day equipment, particularly dimmer controls, a considerable range of lighting styles is available without incurring undue cost. The subject of theatre lighting is intriguingly balanced between technological skill and its artistic application. When one of these two elements is ignored, the quality of the resulting work suffers. No area of theatre must be allowed to become an isolated mystique, but lack of application to the technical procedures will either weaken the quality of productions or serve to inhibit the potential contribution which the *lighting consultant* should make to the whole undertaking. For a thorough treatment of the subject refer to *The Art of Stage Lighting* by Frederick Bentham. It will take the reader from the opening of Richard D'Oyly Carte's new Savoy Theatre in London, in 1881, to a glossary of current equipment. Be as ready to challenge some of his opinions as he is to trail his coat; but expect an entertaining and highly readable book, over-flowing with concern for the practice of theatre.

Modern lighting equipment is not difficult to use. Many lanterns are made which can be used either in fine focus or full flood. The choice of colour media is as wide as a painter's palette. The way to learn about this is readily available: take a lamp and experiment. The experience of others will be valuable, but the effective use of the equipment depends upon direct experience of its behaviour and characteristics. Two pitfalls are: the casual advice of those who have not troubled to learn (everybody feels free to comment on the lighting), and also the habits and procedures which result from too much attention to theatre practice and rely too little upon direct observation. Lighting and set design must be conceived with both in mind. This is particularly relevant when the reproduction of natural-istic effects is required. The shapes and colours of the scenery may do much to facilitate lighting. The important factors are the skills of those involved. An experienced scene painter can provide a completely convincing appearance of shadows and moulded reliefs, while lighting from the wrong angle could wash away the fruits of expensive carpentry or plaster-work.

A prime difficulty of present theatre practice is the decline in painting skill. A few specialists survive, but a sharp reaction against painted scenery in recent years has discouraged appren-ticeship; and this kind of painting can be learned only while working beside an experienced craftsman. The theatre's tendency towards pendulum swings of taste and style may well cost the next generation dearly in this respect. Few will long for everything to be painted on canvas again; but the combination of skilled painting and materials that can be vividly shaped and modelled can provide the most rewarding complement to sensitive lighting.

The essence of imaginative lighting design is the selection and manipulation of space by means of intensity and/or colour. By using considerable intensity it is possible to produce lighting effects in the air alone, but it is a normal assumption that light will be interesting theatrically only when it hits a person or an object. The effect is controlled from the direction, or angle, from which the light approaches its target as much as from sheer brightness or colour. Certain plays or productions, like opera and ballet, call for considerable emphasis upon visual effect, possibly accompanied by music, but not involving the sound of words, at least from many of the performers much of the time. In these cases, low levels of lighting can conjure the imagination without much difficulty. However, this kind of effect will soon become monotonous, even soporific, unless it is well contrasted with quite different lighting either elsewhere on the stage or in the sequence of the show. There is no more important element in lighting than contrast. At its easiest and most obvious, a solitary figure struck by one shaft of light, especially diagonally from behind, must 'work' for a moment. As soon as the figure moves, or speaks or sings, problems will arise. If he does none of these a further problem of monotony will emerge. It is an inevitable result of under-lighting spoken theatre that the actors seem to be inaudible. Situations requiring low-key lighting should be allowed their proper effect: the answer is not just to brighten, but to achieve the maximum clarity through contrast. The seeming inaudibility can occur if a quite strong directional light leaves the speaker's features in gloom. The modelling of strong shadows and highlights may be quite beguiling from a few feet, but the customer may well be getting poorer value. The cinema has a strong advantage over the theatre in this kind of situation. Its lighting is set up for each shot and can be delicately balanced as for close-up; it can also be assumed that the intensity of eventual projection will make the same effect appreciable from the furthest seat in the smokiest cinema.

The acceptability of conscious effect in theatre lighting will depend not only on the work in question but on the general style of the production. As with any element of the show, it must not obstruct or conflict with other contributions: with that proviso, sensitively observed, it will be fruitful to explore the distinctive effects that imaginative lighting can achieve. Overdiscreet lighting may not only be boring, but can also do harm by default, in not shaping or phrasing the mood and space of the production.

Words on pages are a long way from the behaviour of light. The essential step is to experiment. See how much can be done with how little. This is no puritan homily: the problems of unwanted light increase with every lantern used. Keep the difficulties under control, step by step. Contrast, definition and clarity are the vital objectives. Direction, intensity and colour are the means.

A closely parallel function of importance in any production is the province of the *sound technician*. Sound, at its simplest, is the natural voice of the actor or singer: at its most complex, it could be a delicately blended mixture of the human voice, given added reverberation or other re-inforcement, and 'naturally' produced effects, taped effects, orchestral instruments, electronic music, or whatever device that money and skill can provide. Few productions, outside opera, actually demand complexity of sound, yet there is no reason for undervaluing the opportunities which modern equipment can offer.

The question of quality is central where sound is concerned. Scratchy records and tinny speakers used to commend themselves for little more than a convincing impression of bacon frying in the wings. Tapes and electronic developments have opened the world of recording to all. In one respect, the sheer volume of sound, or output power, required by a large theatre separates theatre equipment from domestic tape recorders. Little else does, with the result that skill and experience with the most modest tape machine will contribute towards work on the 'sound' of a production.

Although one may try to categorize types of sound in production, here is another area in which definitions over-lap. The noise of a car arriving may ostensibly be to impart information, to announce the entry of a character; yet, suitably timed it could heighten tension, or bring relief, or simply drown an actor's lines. Bird song may indicate a country setting, even requiring the precise information conveyed by selecting a lark, or a cuckoo, or an owl. The thrumming of sounds on a sultry summer's day may have much more relevance to the mood or atmosphere of the scene than any concern for naturalism.

Music, too, can contribute in more than one way at a time. The script may require an off-stage orchestra, as part of an imagined ball-room in the wings; however, the actual music played not only suggests a great deal about the period, the size of the hall and the style of the dances, but also closely affects the performance of the scene being enacted on stage. Gay music may comment ironically on a contrasting mood, or it may simply destroy the scene; often this judgment can only be made by rehearsal and experiment.

If the director has outlined his requirements for a sound expert to investigate and carry out, a far more creative contribution can result from the 'sound man being given sufficient freedom. The sound expert's research and collection of material will suggest ideas which could not have been thought of in advance. What will count is skill and resource with his equipment as well as awareness of the production's needs. No degree of skill can compensate for inadequate equipment. It is not essential in most theatres to provide highly sophisticated control gear, although a high ratio of returns is enjoyed from well-designed operating desks. But there must be speakers and amplifiers capable of carrying sound at high quality over a great distance. The critical test may not be the ability to carry the sound of state trumpeters or the imaginary orchestra up left; much more likely it will be the ability to suggest the sound of water lapping or an aeroplane passing low over head. These extremes must be catered for, or hours of frustrated work will result. This point is stressed because too often a fear of expense encourages the acceptance of a lower standard. Quality and intensity are subject to close comparison with the pop music scene, and the theatre must not allow bad habits to be accepted as traditions or conventions.

Logically, of course, music is part of sound. In another sense, music can become a major element in a production without ever being 'justified' or in any way part of the plot or situation. Television and films have no inhibitions in this respect. From highly exploitable title 'themes' to endlessly modulating background scores, their effect can readily be observed in any record shop. Perhaps the theatre is suffering from a reaction to the rather profligate use of music elsewhere. But it would be a pity if this tendency were to harden into regular practice. The public activity, the collective imaginative exercise that live entertainment offers, can only be poorer if deprived of the stimulus of music.

Preferably, the music used in theatre should be especially composed. 'Preferably' must be stressed: the difficulty of finding a composer's fee as well as more for the musicians to play 'live' or to record the music will often prevent this ideal solution. However, provided the appropriate copyright conditions are observed, the use of existing music, if intelligently selected, can make valuable contributions. Possibly the greatest of all these is the freedom of imagination which the music can release. There is no need to be restricted to 'correct' periods in selecting music for a production, provided that the contrast is conscious and that the 'clash' contributes. The music is important for the ears of the audience, who are alive today, and so, even if the rest of a production is 'correct' to its original period setting, a modern score can be entirely appropriate. There is no short-cut answer to how to choose suitable music. The essential ingredients are a wide knowledge of music and the judgment to relate a specific work to the production in hand. Like many of the director's decisions it is largely intuitive. If he is not a musical expert, he can elicit advice and suggestions from others: but the director must judge, and 'want' the music he finally selects. It will thus become part of the production.

As the various departments converge towards the final stages of rehearsal, the role of the *technical director* will be seen most clearly. Of course his work has begun long ago, in the earliest stages of planning the production. He will probably have taken charge of ordering materials for the costume designer or of hiring wigs and properties. He will have watched progress on the construction of the settings and generally 'liaised' with everyone concerned with technical aspects of the production. By dress rehearsals he will have taken over the actual control of schedules, relating set-building time to painting, lighting, plotting of sound effects and anything else to do with the mechanics of the show. The importance of this is two-fold: first, that the production comes together as a single unit, ready to take on its own life, independent of detailed direction; and second, that at that most concentrated period of rehearsal the director can give proper attention to the actors. If the director cannot delegate this technical direction, he will have to desert the cast at a time when they most want his attention. A familiar definition of a director is 'an audience of one'. He will be a most unhelpful audience if he is scribbling notes throughout on a mass of minor details.

It is worth emphasizing here that much of the stress of the last rehearsals is imposed by too late provision of the full physical detail of a production. While actors may have been concentrating for weeks, technical operators and stage staff may be meeting tasks at dress rehearsal for the first time. Financial reasons may operate here, but the artistic effect of this kind of schedule is often far more serious than many realize.

Having considered some of the major elements of the total production, it is time to give attention to the work done by the director with the actors. This is not the place for detailed study, for all descriptions of the director in this basic task will tend to express a specific theatrical philosophy and approach. There are numerous accounts available which are the fruits of individual experience and apply to individual theatres or working situations. We are here concerned with more general description and an introduction to the kind of work that is involved.

In any rehearsal situation the director must first establish two things: one, an atmosphere in which the actors can work; and two, the basic intention or point of view of the play which he proposes. The detailed ways of executing these tasks will vary according to all the human factors involved. Some directors like giving a sort of party into which the first reading can be slipped, like a pill inside a sugar coating; they do this because they consider that an easy, personal relationship must precede serious work, that all the defences and susceptibilities of nervous actors will block communication and hinder rehearsal. (Maybe: but it is usually the directors who take most care of this who want eventually to do the most persuading.) Others will adopt a diametrically opposite technique: arrive just in time for the first rehearsal session and after the merest, politest courtesies plunge straight into a lecture on how the play will be done. Yet others will just show a model or sketches of the set and start by 'blocking', or 'plotting', the 'moves'.

One of the greatest misconceptions of the director's work is that he is primarily a traffic controller sent to steer actors round the stage so that they do not collide (except when so required). In fast-working (under-rehearsed) repertory conditions or in amateur societies copying more of the bad habits of professionals than the virtues, this 'steerage' direction may take place. What is certain is that it can only achieve superficial effects unless qualified by other methods. Of course, at a point in time, it may be necessary for the director to decide precise positions and movements. What will matter most in determining this is the meaning which the actor is to convey. How to establish this meaning is the essence of the director's work.

The early stages of rehearsal must be equally concerned with allowing the actor a general framework or overall objective as well as with allowing him considerable freedom to explore the characters' thoughts and emotions. The words which the author has provided are only a fragment of the creation which the actor will eventually offer, and the words will mean little unless they are placed in the proper context. This early, vulnerable, confusing stage is not made any easier by the fact that every actor has a similar problem. During this discovery process the director's help is urgently required – not to provide neat answers, but to offer guide-lines, aids to more discovery, methods of exploring further possibilities.

Some actors have been so trained and accustomed to 'blocking' at the outset that it may avoid a lot of trouble, in the form of cumulative fear, if a quick outline of the physical, mechanical side of the production is offered. Done at some speed, with the clear understanding that everything is subject to change, this can have the effect of getting the company into the water. Then, moving towards alternatives, experiment and improvisation can bring about a creative atmosphere almost unawares. Much depends upon the training and experience of the cast, to say nothing of both in the director.

How to become a director? How to find Sir Tyrone Guthrie's mug? Why should a manager or a society allow anyone to take the first plunge as a director? In the case of a small society it may be that everyone else prefers to act and nobody wants the chore of directing, because this probably also means being stage manager, property borrower and generally overworked task-master. The manager will want further evidence before making the decision. If he is a wise manager, he will look for experience of the theatre's work in other capacities – as actor, stage manager or designer. In addition, he will need assurance that the candidate can present a clear impression of the chosen play and also make it possible for everyone else concerned to work together to achieve this. Unless the apprentice director has a sure foot in at least one area of theatre work, he will have much difficulty in commanding the respect of his colleagues. There are two reasons for this: first, the profession is seriously overcrowded; and second, the actor will eventually have to go on stage and declare himself personally. It will thus be doubly hard for the professional to look respectfully towards a newcomer.

An extra difficulty is that training in direction is relatively hard to get. There are certain processes, particularly a trainee scheme looked after by the Arts Council which gives successful applicants a period of time, usually a year, working in a professional company as a trainee assistant. If all works well, this can be a valuable route: the critical first hurdles can be jumped with artists who are known and understood, and who will not instinctively regard the young director as a stranger. There can also be the valued advice and encouragement from the senior director of the company in support.

It is likely that this process will bring out the emerging ability if it is preceded by other work elsewhere. Before approaching the trainee process, an aspiring director can do much to prepare. Direct involvement in actual work in amateur societies will always contribute. In such work, setting increasingly high standards while maintaining the confidence of colleagues will certainly yield valuable experience. Certain highly exceptional examples of young directors shooting meteorically from university productions into professional work should not confuse the issue here. When actors expect to spend at least two years of hard work training themselves physically, intellectually and emotionally for a gruelling profession, it would be impertinent to recommend short cuts for those who want to control not only young actors but also seasoned artists with more years of working experience than a young director has of age. A conductor is required to be, at least, competent in playing most of the instruments of the orchestra, and a management trainee in commerce or industry may spend several years in a variety of jobs within the firm. This varied training will not guarantee that the young conductor will offer instant inspiration or that the new manager will increase turnover by 500 per cent, but it will ensure that the new man in charge has learned his craft and that he will not easily be deceived or misled into situations where even an experienced director would be absurdly exposed.

Seeing as much professional work (in as many varied styles) as possible is vital. Critical judgment is an essential talent for a director, and this must be formed by his own theatre-going experience, not received at the hands of professional critics. This is not to dismiss professional opinion – far from it – but to stress that what is urgent is to have seen enough theatre to 'know' immediately what is good and bad, right and wrong. The time will come when an actor must be criticized immediately – during rehearsal or just after a show; there will not even be time for a taxi to Fleet Street to prepare the careful phrase.

A university course in drama will allow a valuable concentration upon many important aspects of theatre as well as offering sympathetic circumstances for practical work. Some vocational drama schools offer courses in direction, and universities, especially in the United States, offer similar courses, chiefly on a post-graduate level. In the United Kingdom opportunities for specific directional training are few, but with the profession as overcrowded as it is, there is not likely to be a rush to encourage more applicants than the opportunities for employment can justify.

The pressures that overcrowding exerts will best be counteracted by quality and by systematic preparation. A thoroughly grounded knowledge of the theatre's many crafts, intelligently geared to a sensitive and critical questioning of 'tradition', will offer a chance of survival. The process is not quick. It is not desirable that it should be. Direction is nothing without understanding; and for that one usually has to wait a while.

5

Design and Equipment

Graham Woodruff

The Designer in the Production

A characteristic of twentieth-century stage production is the
synthesis of the various elements of theatre art. Acting,
make-up, costumes, setting, light and sound are carefully
orchestrated by the director in his attempt to achieve a unity
of interpretation. The result is that the designer is no longer
brought in at the last moment merely to ornament a play.
Now he is involved with the reading of the script at the very
beginning of the planning, discussing the actions and motives
of the characters and taking part in the evolution of the production. He has become less of a decorative paper-hanger and
more of a crucial member of an integrated production team.
This synthesis is perhaps best exemplified in the productions
of the Berliner Ensemble since the war and stems from the
influential writings of Adolphe Appia and Gordon Craig at the
turn of the century. Caspar Neher and Karl Von Appen not
only design the costumes and settings at the Berliner Ensemble,
but in dozens of sketches drawn before the rehearsal period
begins, they suggest the positions of the characters and the
physical relationship between them at certain moments in the
play. They are thus concerned with the creation and organization of the scenic space.

In the contemporary theatre, it has become increasingly
difficult to distinguish between what the director and what the
designer have contributed to the final result. Several men are
capable of doing both jobs on their own. Many other directors

and designers work together over a period of years – partnerships that immediately spring to mind are those of Roger Planchon and René Allio in France and Jerzy Grotowski and Jerzy Gurawski in Poland.

Before Appia and Craig, the scene designer tended to be isolated from the actor. The architecture of the Georgian

Fig. 1   What Will My Settings Make the Actors *Do*?

theatre – a curious combination of the Italianate proscenium arch and the Elizabethan thrust stage – encouraged this independence. The forestage on which the actors performed was so far removed from the space used for displaying the scenery that the scene painter was tempted to work for his own ends. What he often produced was a series of flat scenes, delightfully painted but forming little more than a background to the actors. The Duke of Saxe-Meiningen, a German prince who

H

formed and ran his own company in the second half of the nineteenth century, was one of the first to establish that no setting had an existence independent from the actor and that the scenic effects must be related to the actors' movements. His drawings were revolutionary, because they were not pictures with settings but almost always settings filled with actors. They rejected the limitations of the two-dimensional painted back-cloth and integrated platforms and steps into the setting so that the actors could move on and around them (Fig. 1). Saxe-Meiningen's concern was to visualize how his settings would affect the movements of the actors and the spatial relationships between them. Such an emphasis on the actor is fundamental to contemporary design: 'You should start with the actor's face and pay attention to that. Then comes what he looks like from head to toe. Then comes what he sits on, hides behind or handles.'[1] Through light, colour, shape, line, mass, scale and texture, the designer's aim is to intensify the visual effect of the actor.

There is a further implication in the work of Saxe-Meiningen. Three-dimensional design influences the human activity it embraces by its plan as well as by its façade. The position of a raised platform and its spatial relationship to other structures and furnishings, the size of the acting area it creates and the height and width of the steps leading to it are all factors shaping the movement of the actors. An audience is particularly aware of the plan of a design when it watches the play from above the acting area as in the Greek classical theatre at Epidauros. But even when unseen by the audience, the plan controls the movement patterns of the actors, while the façade expresses the prevailing mood of the players as they move through those patterns.

The Style of the Design

Theatre design books published in the 1920s and '30s tend to concentrate their discussion on style. In doing so, they try to pigeon-hole designers into schools of historical realism, naturalism, stylized realism, surrealism, expressionism, symbolism, constructivism, formalism, etc. In the contemporary theatre it is more difficult to do this. Designers work nowadays on a wide variety of productions from the dramatic, operatic and ballet repertoire, and each show demands a fresh and original approach. Even so, certain stylistic trends can be indicated.

The historical realism and naturalism of the nineteenth century have disappeared except in the most unimaginative and stultified theatres. The main function of historical realism is to indicate the precise time and place for the action. The audience is told that the stage represents Bavaria or Hellenic Greece, in ancient or modern times, royal boudoir or working class kitchen, summer sunshine or winter snow. No matter whether the play is comedy or tragedy, satire or fantasy, the designer brings on to the stage the results of careful research. For his production of *Sardanapalus*, Charles Kean made use of recent archeological discoveries and of treasures in the British Museum so that his scenes would represent an accurate reconstruction of ancient Nineveh. In 1853 he was rewarded by his election to the Royal Society of Antiquarians. Going to the Princess Theatre in the nineteenth century was as important a way of learning facts as a guided tour through a museum.

Scenic naturalism also involved an imitation of life. Its value was that it presented a real environment in which real modern people could be shown and analysed. It is no coincidence that the furniture for André Antoine's first production at the Théâtre Libre in 1897 was taken to the theatre straight from his dining room. Antoine believed that a stage design, whether landscape or interior, should always be based on an existing natural setting. If it was an interior, he planned the set with its four walls and did not worry initially about the audience's viewpoint. Exits were chosen with due regard to architectural accuracy, and the hallways and rooms connecting these exits were included in the design. Only then, after examining the interior from every angle, did he choose exactly where he wanted the 'fourth' wall. The naturalistic setting attempted to produce the same visual effect as the photographic image. Indeed, we have discovered that the camera does it far more successfully, and in this century the cinema and television media have taken over the world of naturalism. The consequence has been that designers in the theatre have for the most part abandoned attempts to produce settings of this kind and have instead sought to reflect reality either through the symbol or by a stylization of reality.

Perhaps the most influential advocate of symbolism is Gordon Craig. Writing at the beginning of the twentieth century, Craig describes a design method in which there are no 'authentic' settings or costumes. His approach is to forget the details of actuality and to create the mood of the play through line, shape or colour. Such a setting seeks to be evocative rather than descriptive. Craig had this to say about planning a design for *Macbeth*:

> I see two things. I see a lofty and steep rock, and I see the moist cloud which envelopes the head of this rock. That is to say, a place for fierce and warlike men to inhabit, and a place for phantoms to nest in.[2]

The rock and the moist cloud, with the brown and grey colours that characterize them, dominate Craig's settings for the play. For the production of *Macbeth* in 1921, the American designer Robert Edmond Jones followed the same method, choosing the shape of a dagger as the dominant symbol of the play. So the designer listens to the rhythms of the play in order to create a relevant mood and atmosphere, not because they are important in themselves, but because the mood of a setting can reinforce important aspects of the play.

Realistic design in the contemporary theatre has also rejected the photographic image and is more concerned with presenting realistic elements rather than the complete picture. In this style of design, the greatest influence is to be found in the work of the Berliner Ensemble. This company, whose visit to England in 1956 had a profound effect on our theatre, adapted naturalism to serve, in particular, the plays of the German playwright Bertolt Brecht. His designers had no use for symbolism, which expressed general ideas, nor could they turn back to the naturalistic stage with its mixture of the relevant and the trivial. Just to copy reality was not enough: reality needed to be not only recognized but also understood in a clear and fresh light. Brecht had the close co-operation of his designers in all the visual elements of production at the Berliner Ensemble. The settings of Caspar Neher and Karl Von Appen are characterized by grey, subdued colours and worn or weather-beaten materials and textures. In their choice of furniture and properties, they were concerned with exact detail:

> With what care Neher selects a chair . . . and it all affects the playing. One chair will have short legs and the height of the accompanying table will also have to be calculated, so that whoever eats at it has to take up a quite specific attitude, and the conversation of these people as they bend more than usual when eating takes on a different character, which makes an episode clearer.[3]

The reason for this concern about the choice of furniture is clear, since every detail affects the way the characters behave and how they relate to each other. Brecht was also insistent that the small hand properties such as weapons, instruments, purses, cutlery, etc., were always authentic and able to pass the closest scrutiny. This emphasis on the right property or piece of furniture can be seen in our contemporary theatre. For *The War of the Roses*, John Bury searched for an object for every situation – a cannon, a throne, a bishop's chair – and this object became the dominating scenic element in the scene.

But when it came to the architecture, Brecht's designers were content to give indications of the locality. A blue strip of material on the stage presented a river; one door and part of a wall indicated a room, though the piece of wall that was there was sometimes made of bricks and mortar instead of canvas and paint. A further point is the emphasis placed on the theatre building and its stage conventions. Against a neutral background which was usually the cyclorama of the theatre and in a white light which left no room for mystery or magic, the technical apparatus of the theatre remained unconcealed. Lighting instruments were visible, scene changes were made in view of the audience and slide projections were used to emphasize or clarify the action. In *The Days of the Commune*, for example, Von Appen used a drawing of Paris in 1871 as a scenic background.

René Allio's designs for Gogol's *Dead Souls* are a clear example of the Brechtian influence on contemporary design (Fig. 2, see p. 110). Upstage there is a vast landscape with a sky-line of indistinguishable forms and figures. Immediately in front of the landscape is hung a large picture which is an enlargement of a fragment of the horizon. On either side of the stage there are periaktoi* which serve to emphasize the social and topographical character of the main scenic element. The façade of a typical embassy house accompanies the scenes that take place in the governor's house, and for the scenes set in the countryside the periaktoi turn to reveal a tree with a ladder leaning against it. Finally, downstage centre is the main scenic element,

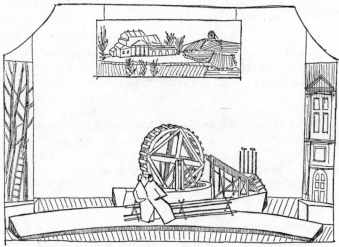

Fig. 2   The Setting and Its Environment

which in most scenes is a full-scale enlargement of part of the picture hung at the rear. It is three-dimensional and realistic, though certain elements may be simplified. The total effect of the landscape, the picture, the periaktoi and the main scenic element is to emphasize the relationship of the set to its environment.

Environment or Machine?

The creation of a suitable environment or meaningful mood

* Three flats battened together in the shape of a triangle so that they can be revolved to reveal each of the flats in turn.

for the action of the play is not universally accepted as being necessary for a stage design. Some designers believe that the setting should belong to the stage and the actor, rather than to the play. They care nothing for mood and advocate the elimination of all features that are not absolutely functional and specifically needed for stage business. The aim is rather to create structures which give the maximum intensity to the movement of the actors. The stronghold of this design method

Fig. 3   A Machine for Acting

is to be found in Russia in the productions of Meyerhold and Tairov. Meyerhold's setting for *The Magnanimous Cuckold* is composed of bare structural forms arranged to allow for an uninterrupted flow of action. The various platforms, ramps, steps and ladders allow the actor a variety of positions at various levels, and the supports are purposely exposed to reveal posts and beams (Fig. 3).

The constructivist sculptors had led the way into these abstract mechanical structures, using wire, glass and metal. Meyerhold brought the movement into the theatre and developed a theory of acting, called 'Biomechanics', which encouraged the actors to use the setting like acrobats. In the contemporary theatre, the influence of Meyerhold's designs and acting theory is still powerful. The setting for the Living Theatre's recent production of *Frankenstein* is similar in style, employing tubular scaffolding poles to construct a three-storey acting machine.

Kinetic Scenery

One of the most productive areas of development in contemporary scenic design has been in kinetic scenery. Joseph Svoboda, in particular, has been exploring ways to produce an active setting which moves and develops with the play and the actor. Interesting experiments in this direction were made by Craig in his projects called *The Steps* and *Scene*. Craig had the idea of dividing the stage floor and ceiling into chess-boards and making each square rise and lower. Thus the space became endlessly variable, with the floor and ceiling making stairways, platforms, seats, thick walls and wide spaces. Several variations of this scheme were produced by Craig in etchings which he called 'moods for movement'. They are not intended to be interpretations of particular plays but show how a single assembly of mobile units are capable of infinite adaptation.

Of course, moving scenery is by no means a new phenomenon. Theatre architects in the court theatres of the Italian Renaissance designed scenes which revolved or slid to the side to reveal others. For three hundred years the basic method of scene changing in the English theatre was to run off painted flats along grooved tramways in order to discover another series of flats behind them. Flying apparatus and traps for elevating scenery from the basement are also traditional machines.

But in the twentieth century, technicians have developed various ways to make the stage itself move. Elevators and sliding and revolving stages have provided us with three ways to achieve this. The stage can be built in sections on lifts so that a complete setting can be prepared below stage and then raised into position while the set it replaces is lowered, struck and reset. A simpler device will be used in the new Barbican Theatre, which will have two lifts upstage left and right to bring up sets from the scene dock below. Formerly worked by winch or counterweight hoist on the same principle as the sash window, lifts are now operated by electrical or hydraulic means.

For sliding stages to be incorporated into the stage proper there has to be considerable wing space, which is often lacking in English theatres. An alternative is to use rostra on wheels which can be rolled onstage from the wings. But perhaps the most effective machine is the revolve, which enables the designer to construct a permanent structure that is seen from various angles during the performance, like a sculpture that one walks around. He can then add elements lowered from the flies or brought in on trucks. For Lionel Bart's *Oliver*, Sean Kenny used a revolve, two side trucks which ran around the perimeter of the revolve and a variety of flying pieces. In this way he was able to produce elaborate settings with a simple basic plan.

Joseph Svoboda has been exploring scenic movement towards and away from the audience. His designs for *Hamlet*, for example, show a complex of steps, walls, platforms and doorways which move backwards and forwards 'like the secret drawers in a Louis Quinze writing desk'.[4] He uses the same idea for *Romeo and Juliet*, where the balcony is particularly effective as it advances and recedes into the darkness upstage created by back lighting and the black background. But Svoboda's sets are not bogged down with over-complex machinery. Those at the National Theatre in Prague have to be capable of being changed from one day to the next and sometimes between the matinee and the evening performance. He works in a conventional proscenium theatre, and he is the master of the traditional and simple means of stage transformation.

Svoboda's experiments in scenic kinetics have aimed at combining traditional theatre methods with those of the film. He wants a stage which can change its form and structure depending on its needs and content. The use of projection, for example, combines a projected image with a three-dimensional stage, and a live three-dimensional actor with his two-dimensional projected image. The elements of theatrical production have been traditionally understood as actor, make-up, costume, scenery, lighting and sound. Now, we find the full scale use of electronics, including film, television, taped sound and projected still images. The Polyvision and Diapolyecran rooms at the Czechoslovakian Pavilion at Expo 67 demonstrated new kinds of film and still environments that can serve both as a scenic background and indeed as an independent performing element. These techniques, which were based on ideas of Svoboda, have been developed by Jaroslav Fric, who is chief of research and engineering for the Prague Scenic Institute. The Polyvision was the total conversion of a medium-sized, rather high room into a film and slide environment. Mirrors, moving cubes and prisms, and projections from both outside the space and from within the cubes, all built up the feeling of a space of great flexibility. The ten-minute presentation used 11 film projectors, 28 slide projectors and a 10-track computer tape for programming. The Diapolyecran was restricted to one wall, with the audience sitting on the floor, and involved a simultaneous projection of slides on a mosaic projection screen consisting of 112 projection surfaces. The surfaces were projected on from behind and they could be changed singly, in groups, or all at once. Each surface was mounted on a steel frame that had three positions so that the images could be thrust out towards the audience or moved back away from it. The total effect was of a constantly changing mosaic of projected pictures.

These inventions have been incorporated into theatrical practice by a piece of apparatus which Svoboda calls 'The Magic Lantern'. This enables him to move a projected image about the stage and to surround the actor with past, present or future, or fragments of all three merged together. In this way, Svoboda moves scenery around the actor, altering perspectives for the audience and presenting more than one image of the play's action at the same time.

New Materials in Scenic Design

The traditional theatre materials of wood and painted canvas are now being used with more discretion. Wood will do almost anything you ask of it in the way of framework, but metal will do more because it can be bent or welded to any shape and still retain its strength. Tubular scaffolding, in particular, can be effective, especially when a wide span or bridge would demand impossibly heavy joists if made of wood. We are fast moving away from the world of painted canvas. The contemporary scene designer is now 'light years away from the omnipresent stage-painter who would have said: "Steel, laddy? Right – a bit of white paint, a bit of black, a bit of silver – there's steel for you".'[5] Paint-shops are becoming more concerned with creating and texturing surfaces than painting them, and even when wood is used it is often treated rather than painted. In Farrah's set for *The Three Sisters*, the solid timber setting was burnt with blowlamps, rather than painted, to get the effect of great age. Then the timber was scrubbed down to get rid of the burns and to bring out the grain. The final effect of a hundred-year-old piece of flaking timber could not have been achieved with paint.

Designers are now concerned with finding new surfaces that are the right weight, density and reflective index in addition to the right colour. For *The War of the Roses* at Stratford, Bury used sheets of copper leaf which were stained and treated with chemicals. Other popular metals available are bronze, tin, gold and silver sheets as well as wire netting and iron and aluminium tubing and sections. The range of natural materials used includes cork, untanned leather, plaited straw, rush, reed and osier. Besides, a whole range of synthetic materials have come on to the market. Latex, formica, astralon, celon, fibreglass, plexiglass and jablite have the advantage of being light and durable and give an excellent impression of solidity. Polystyrene is frequently used even though it causes trouble with certain local fire officers responsible for theatre safety. The advantages of this dry foam plastic are that it is as light as a feather, will absorb paint and can be cut clean with a fine-toothed saw or a heated knife. There are also a group of synthetic rubbers with which it is well worth experimenting. Some of them can be sprayed, some layed on with a trowel, and others first moulded and then glued to the surface which requires treatment. Besides, there are new fabrics such as terylene, nylon, imitation leather, artificial jute, down net, fur, etc. However, these new materials do not exclude the imaginative use of more familiar and homely materials such as rope, egg trays, hose pipe, stove piping, lead pipe, cardboard boxes, newspapers, cellophane, silver paper and photographic paper.

The Scenic Institute in Prague, under the inspiration of Miroslav Kouril, has been in the forefront of experiment with new materials. New plastics have enabled Czechoslovakian designers to improve the use of lighting and especially to provide projection surfaces which permit the reflection of light in the precise direction required. In *Hamlet*, Svoboda used movable panels of black plastic to throw reflected light into parts of the stage where direct lighting could not be reached. Svoboda also attempts to make the floor of the stage as dark as possible from the point of view of the audience. This he achieves by using ridged rubber which casts shadow towards the audience and reflects the light upstage. In this way the reflected light does not detract from the basic effect of the setting.

Lighting

This concern for efficient reflecting surfaces reveals the interest of the contemporary designer in stage lighting. Indeed, it is essential for a designer to have a sound knowledge of the effect of direction and intensity of light, the theory of light colour, the principles of acting area and blending light, and the interplay of light and texture. The fact that materials can change their quality under light is well illustrated by Peter Brook's production of *King Lear* in which the expensive, carefully made leather costumes looked like plastic until they were textured. But once this knowledge of lighting is acquired, the designer can achieve settings with an absolute minimum of strictly scenic elements. An empty space plunged into darkness becomes the starting point for lighting in the modern theatre. The art then consists of putting light where you want it and taking it away from where you don't want it. Light, even more than scenery, shapes the action and exerts an hypnotic control over the interest and the emotions of the audience. A severe limitation of most illustrations of stage design is that they are not able to take into account the effect of changing light.

Light is the one theatrical element which has improved during the twentieth century. The age of electricity has perfected an art that started thousands of years ago when actors danced to the flames of a forest fire. Most Greek, Mediaeval and Elizabethan performances took place in the daytime, and the Greeks certainly knew how to make use of the sun and the open sky. But the Romans knew the effects that could be achieved at night with torches. And when the architect-designers of the Italian Renaissance constructed playhouses indoors, they revealed considerable understanding of the principles of stage lighting. Chandeliers were used to illuminate the auditorium, and glass lamps, filled with various coloured liquids, were concealed just behind the proscenium border, behind backcloths and on the back of flats onstage. They realized that the stage lighting appeared more brilliant and attracted more attention if the auditorium was darkened, and they also made use of atmospheric lighting in tragedies, beginning with a brightly lit stage and then lowering tin cylinders suspended by wires over every lamp to dim or extinguish the lights at the catastrophe of the play. The introduction of gas lighting at the beginning of the nineteenth century brought a greater concentration of light onto the stage, and the intensity was subject to a certain control. But stage lighting still consisted mainly of flat, general glare from long rows of open flames, and it was only with the invention of the incandescent lamp in 1879 that the real development of modern lighting began. The incandescent lamp is safe, noiseless, available in many sizes and easily controlled by a dimmer. The filament is so concentrated that, with a reflector and lens, it creates a pool of directional, not diffused, light. It is also easy to put a sheet of colour medium in front of the lens. So light now has shape, direction and colour, and can easily change from bright to dim.

The great prophet of the new art of lighting was Adolphe Appia, who was the first to state that the designer must not only plan his setting as an architectural and pictorial composition but must at the same time visualize it under light. This is now accepted as a general principle of design. Appia argued that the stage should no longer be a flat picture against which the actor gestures, but a three-dimensional area of ramps and platforms through which the actor moves. He rejected the practice of flooding the stage with light and instead suggested light that gave true relief to the scenic architecture and that emphasized the actor. The acting areas were contracted or expanded by fluctuations of light according to the emotional key of the scene, so that the light illuminated the successive moods – hope, fear, pity, resignation, ecstasy, despair – of the dramatic plot as it was played.

In recent years there have been further improvements in lighting equipment. The designer now has greater control over the intensity, size, shape, colour and quality of the beam of light that comes from the lantern. Significant advances have also been made in control systems in order to simplify the procedure of setting and operating light cues. The latest development is the Instant Dimmer Memory board, which records electronically each cue as it is set and can play the cue back any time. The cues for an entire production can be stored on a drum, and it is possible to envisage a theatre having a library of reels containing light plots of all the productions performed there. Each reel can then be reinserted into the computer system when the play returns to the repertoire.

Designing in New Theatre Forms

Modern lighting has simplified stage design. It has also made obsolete the old painted picture-stage and its proscenium frame. Instead of standing in front of a distant, painted backcloth, the actor now moves in, on and around three-dimensional structures. The proscenium arch, wing flats and side walls fade into darkness as acting areas are defined by pools of light. The plastic stage was developed within the proscenium theatre, but it made the proscenium arch irrelevant. The desire today is to be rid of the paraphernalia of the picture stage and to view the three-dimensional qualities of the theatre as one views a sculpture. This is impossible in most of the existing buildings in England, which were built in the nineteenth or early twentieth century. These theatres originate from the Italian Renaissance and are based on the principle of two separate rooms facing each other: the stage, enclosed and framed; and the auditorium, shaped like a horseshoe and based on Court hierarchy, with the best seat in the middle of the first circle. The irony is that this architectural form was originally designed to accommodate action within the horseshoe, with the end stage reserved for spectacular scenic effects. But apart from isolated experiments such as Astley's amphitheatre, the action has since been restricted to the raised stage, and for nearly 300 years we have been faced with the paradoxical situation of the three-dimensional actor moving against a two-dimensional setting. The Italianate theatre cannot be modernized. It is completely outdated: 'It is like a great hysterical Victorian birdcage standing between the man who writes the poem and the man who listens.'[6] The essential core of the theatre is live actors in the presence of a live audience, and it is this relationship between actor and audience that has been the main concern of designers of our new theatres. New spatial relationships have been established, so that the presence of the actor is more strongly felt and the contribution of the audience increased. The designer has returned to his former role of architect.

The most modest change is to eliminate the proscenium arch and form an open end stage with the auditorium remaining almost unchanged. The Mermaid Theatre at Blackfriars and the Phoenix Theatre, Leicester, are post-war examples of this form. Both theatres have revolves to effect changes of scenery, but the basic conventions of setting in this form of theatre need not, in fact, be any different from those of the proscenium theatre. An interesting variant of the open end stage is the Vieux-Colombier, which has a permanent architectural setting (Fig. 4, see p. 120). This theatre represents a simple and austere reaction to the lush costumes and settings of Bakst and Diaghilev. Jacques Copeau, the first director of the Vieux-Colombier, used the formal architecture of the stage as the basis for all his settings and then made minor changes such as the addition of properties or draperies and the insertion of doors and windows.

Several new theatres have stages which thrust out into the auditorium so that they are surrounded by the audience on three sides. Some of these also have architectural backgrounds. The theatre at Stratford, Ontario, for example, makes no concession to scenery but offers a formal background of entrances and steps and a pavilion with columns supporting a platform above. There are many historical precedents for the thrust stage in Greece, Rome, Elizabethan England, China, Japan and India, and in all there tends to be an architectural background. This form of stage encourages the director to explore three-dimensional choreography which can be particularly effective when the seating for the audience is raised above the acting area. But the emphasis is invariably on the actor, and this is where the designer starts, considering the actor's clothes and properties before his surroundings.

In the arena stage, too, the designer is mainly concerned with the actor. Theatre-in-the-round tends to demand a simplicity of

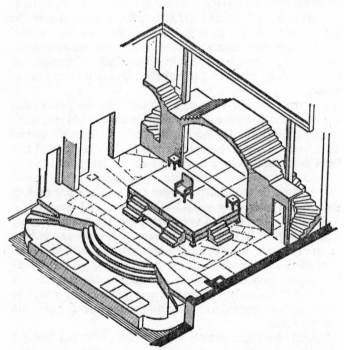

Fig. 4   The Basis of the Setting Is the Theatre Architecture Itself

furnishing, but among the opportunities offered to the designer are suspended and transparent scenery. The stage floor is another scenic area which tends to be used, as in Peter Cheeseman's production of *The Knotty* which the Victoria Theatre (Stoke) Company performed on a large map illustrating the various routes of the South Staffordshire Railway.

The traverse stage, which divides the audience into two, is ideal for plays with powerful conflict and allows for elaborate scenic buildings or structures at either end of the acting area. The caliper stage, on the other hand, envelopes the audience and allows the designer to plan for simultaneous action and peripheral vision. At the Ruth Taylor Theatre in Dallas, three stages surround the auditorium so that a changing relationship between actor and audience can be achieved. The first ten rows are on swivel chairs which make it possible to experience a change in perspective from a close-up view of one stage, then an adjustment to a long view of a second, and a different view of a third stage. Peripheral vision is therefore possible, whereby the main event on one stage is augmented by contrasting events in other areas.

There are alternatives to the theatre that establishes a fixed spatial relationship between actor and audience. One is to build a flexible theatre which can be adapted to a variety of forms according to the demands made by each play. This has been difficult to achieve, and several adaptable theatres in England have proved to be compromise solutions for one or all of their forms. Perhaps the Octagon Theatre, Bolton, is the most successful attempt so far, and this is probably because the architect did not try to include a proscenium stage and a fly-tower. But three main forms – open, thrust and arena – have been achieved, the latter two with particular success (Fig. 5, see p. 122). A second alternative to a fixed form is for the architect to provide an empty space in which there is complete freedom to design new actor-audience relationships:

> In theatre architecture, you've got to be sure that you don't make any definite statements. It may be a total exaggeration but, ideally, theatres should be built of paper. If you want to build a space that's mouldable each time for whatever you want to put into it, you can't build great re-inforced concrete beams. In this time of great metamorphosis, the best thing is to design a giant envelope, sound proof it, heat it, and inside it let the activity happen and design it in such a way that permits the activity to change all the time.[7]

The small studio at the University of Texas attempts to provide such a space. The floor is sixty feet square and divided into ten-foot square units that can be lowered or raised by a jack in the basement. The ceiling, similarly divided and suspended

I

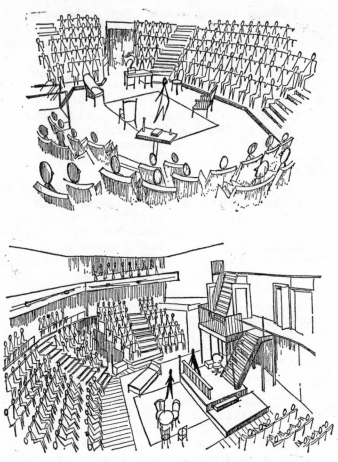

Fig. 5   An Adaptable Theatre

from the roof structure, forms a grid for stage lighting and suspended scenery. The addition of adjustable walls provides a flexible space which allows the designer considerable freedom to create a unique environment for the individual play.

This merging of the roles of scene designer and theatre architect is a striking feature of contemporary design. The designer who is involved in the planning of a theatre building can influence not only the style of production but also the whole policy of the theatre. An interesting illustration of this is Stephen Joseph's brief to the architect for a 'Fish and Chip' theatre (Fig. 6). The brief is to build a theatre-in-the-round

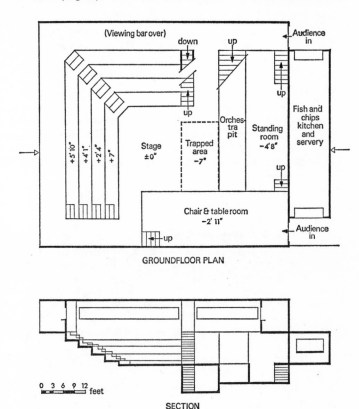

GROUNDFLOOR PLAN

SECTION

Fig. 6   The Designer Can Influence the Policy of a Theatre

accommodating 400 people. The special requirements include a rectangular stage that has rising rows of seats on two sides, a low-standing pit on the third side and a dining-room level on the fourth. All around the theatre, above the level of the back row, there is a viewing bar, arranged so that the audience can sit for a drink and snack and watch the play at the same time. Joseph continues in his brief:

> Kitchens and serveries and bars are to be provided, offering a limited range of refreshments, including fish and chips, soups and rolls, salad bowls, buns, cakes, biscuits, fruit, nuts, ice-cream, beer, coffee, tea, soft drinks and wine. Serve yourself at the counter. All sections of the auditorium should be organically connected to encourage free flow of audience from one place to another, even during performance. The design should be asymmetrical and invite movement. The seats should be generously spaced. Proportions so related to human stature that the actors and audience dominate the building and not the other way round. . . . The viewing bar should be a good rowdy place, and therefore acoustically separated from the restricted area. It should have sound reinforcement from the stage through a series of loud-speakers, locally controlled; plus jacks for headphones which may help deaf people and the occasional attentive person on a particularly noisy pay-day performance.
>
> The stage should be provided with an orchestra pit and a balcony acting level. . . . Ensure that a car can be got on to the stage. Provide for power for, say, a welding demonstration or freezing the floor for an ice show.[8]

Here again is the desire to achieve an intimate and informal relationship between actor and audience. Yet this is not simply a theatre for actors. It is worth noting that when he wrote this brief, Stephen Joseph had already initiated theatre companies in Scarborough and Stoke-on-Trent which are remarkable for their output of new plays.

Interesting experiments which attempt to redefine the spatial relationship between the actor and audience have been carried out by the architect Jerzy Gurawski in close collaboration with Jerzy Grotowski. In several of their productions the actor and the audience share the space (Fig. 7, see p. 125). For *Kordian*, for example, the whole room is built up to suggest the interior of a mental hospital, and the spectators are incorporated into the structure as patients. For *Dr Faustus*, the spectators attend the play as friends at the last supper of Faustus and the play is acted out on long trestle tables. In *The Constant Prince*, the spectators

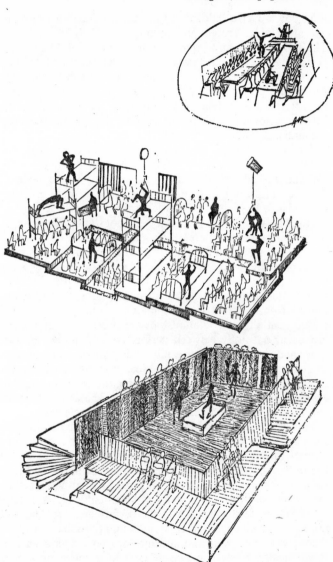

Fig. 7 The Spectators are Incorporated into the Scenic Structure

look down over a balcony, as if on a forbidden act or on an operating table. A recent production of *The Pit* by Inter-Action's The Other Company explores a similar relationship. At the beginning, the four actors are completely enclosed by four walls and the audience spy on them through little windows. As the play progresses and the players reveal their true natures, the barriers are gradually dismantled. By the end, the barriers between actor and audience have gone, the space is clear and the audience come face to face.

A further development is a performance in which there is a constant exchange of space between performer and spectator. To find precedents for this form we have to go back to Mediaeval folk ritual. In performances such as those involving the Padstow horse or the Norwich dragon, the village or place near it was used for the play. But it did not stand still; it ranged over a loosely defined area. The spectators gave way when it approached and then followed when it moved away. A similar atmosphere might have been achieved within a defined space in the Mediaeval performance of *The Castle of Perseverance*, where the audience adjusted their positions as the actors moved from scaffold to scaffold. Once one gives up fixed seating, entirely new relationships are possible. Body contact can occur naturally between performers and audience, voice levels and acting intensities can be widely varied and a sense of shared experience engendered. Most important, each scene creates its own space, either contracting to a remote corner or expanding to fill all the available space. The action breathes and the audience itself becomes a major scenic element.

This idea is illustrated in Naftali Yavin's production of *The Journey*, where the performers and audience join together in a journey through a variety of spaces (Fig. 8, see p. 127). At the beginning, the audience assemble in a long and narrow waiting-room. Their names are taken, and one by one they are summoned to pass through a series of small cubicles where they come face to face with each of the performers. After pausing in a room which enables them to look into the cubicles without themselves being seen, the audience are invited into an end-stage theatre where the players present a satire on certain political and social topics. In the next space, which is constructed like a maze, the actors and audience mingle closely

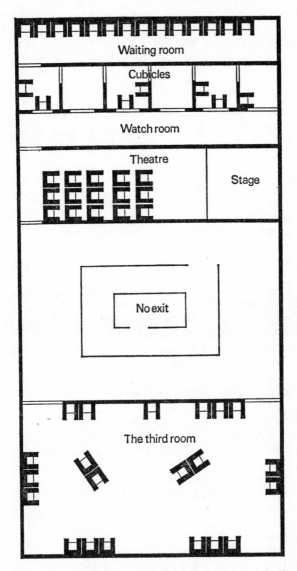

Fig. 8 Constant Exchange of Space Between Actor and Audience

together. Finally, they all move on into a theatre-in-the-round, and here *The Journey* concludes with the audience moving their chairs into the centre of the space and facing each other in two rows.

Freedom and Simplicity

Despite the many inventions and the multiplicity of effects available, there is a desire for simplicity and freedom in contemporary design. Attempts are being made to define the unique quality of theatre art and to discover what separates this activity from other categories of performance such as film and television. Theatre can exist without theatrical costume and stage decoration, without a separate performance area and without artificial lighting and sound effects. Its essence lies in the talent and skill of the live actor performing before a live audience.

This desire for freedom and simplicity and concentration on the art of the actor is expressed in the productions of Jerzy Grotowski. In *Acropolis*, for example, the performance area is shared by the actor and audience, and the setting, which is a metaphor for the Auschwitz concentration camp, has been reduced to objects which are indispensable to the dramatic action. There is no dependence on properties; a certain number of objects are gathered at the beginning, and they are sufficient to handle all the situations of the play. In the middle of the space stands a large rectangular box with stovepipes, a wheelbarrow, a bathtub, nails and hammers heaped on it. Each object has multiple uses: 'The bathtub is a very pedestrian bathtub; on the other hand it is a symbolic bathtub: it represents all the bathtubs in which human bodies were processed for the making of soap and leather.'[9] Turned upside down the bathtub becomes an altar; set in a high place it becomes Jacob's nuptial bed. The wheelbarrows are tools for daily work, but propped against the walls they can also be thrones for Priam and Hecuba. One of the stovepipes is transformed by Jacob's imagination and becomes his bride. Thus the setting and properties are reduced to the barest essentials required to tell the story of the play.

The Designer's Qualifications

There is no compulsory training nor paper qualification necessary to start work as a stage designer in England. A few begin as stage carpenters and learn by assisting in the theatre workshop. Most have had basic art courses at one of the art colleges, and some have taken specialist courses in theatre design either at an art college or at university. Others train for allied professions and come into the theatre as qualified commercial artists, architects, architectural engineers, etc.

But all should have certain qualifications. First, the designer must have an understanding of the history of dramatic production. Each age has created theatre conventions which were acceptable to its own society but which differed, sometimes radically, from those which preceded or followed it. Plays chosen in one season at a theatre might well range from Aeschylus to Arden. Anyone seriously interested in designing for the theatre must know not only its history but also its plays. He must be familiar with plays from all periods and understand the staging conventions that were used when they were first produced.

The designer should have a working knowledge of the related skills in the theatre. The production of a play is a co-operative venture which demands close working relationships, and the more thoroughly he understands the problems facing the director, actor, costume designer, lighting artist and carpenter, the more intelligently he can assist in finding solutions for production problems. Perhaps the most important of these fields is direction. Play analysis, interpretation, mood, style, movement, picturization and composition are some of the aspects of a production that should concern not only the director but the designer as well, since they have a direct bearing on the final form of the setting. It is useful, too, for the designer to have had some experience, however limited, as an actor. The relationship between the actor and his audience is the core of theatre art, and some understanding of this relationship is essential for the designer. He is also much more likely to consider such details as steps that are too high and narrow, ramps with too steep inclines or practical doors and windows that are unreliable if, as an actor, he has personally encountered on stage some of the difficult moments created by poor planning of this kind. I have already mentioned that lighting is one of the designer's most effective tools, and he must know how to use it to realize its full potential. The designer who does not understand how coloured light reacts on coloured pigments and fabrics runs the risk of having the colour scheme of his design unintentionally altered, sometimes with disastrous results. He must also understand period, style and colour of costumes in order to ensure a unity in the setting and costumes.

Within the organization of a production, no relationship is closer than that between the designer and the carpenter. The process of designing and building scenery is no different to that found in any other field where an idea for an object is conceived, put on paper as a sketch, translated into accurate working drawings and finally constructed into a three-dimensional reality. It is clearly important for the carpenter to follow accurately the building specifications and dimensions. However, the study of technical production is not simply a matter of being accomplished in working with workshop tools. The construction of scenery involves problems not always encountered in other types of construction. It must be planned so that it can be built rapidly and inexpensively. As it is built in one place and used in another, it must be easily moved. For convenience in storage and shifting, it is usually constructed in separate pieces, which must be joined and taken apart quickly and easily. A sound knowledge of the intricacies of building, rigging and shifting scenery cannot be ignored by those who design for the theatre.

Finally, the designer must have a genuine interest in people and their environment, the clothes they wear, the houses they live in and the cities and countries they inhabit. He should understand formal and spatial relationships and the value of colour. Most important of all, he must be able to discover the essence of the play in hand and to translate ideas and emotions into visual images.

Notes

1   Christopher Morley, 'The Designer Talks', in *Plays and Players* (January 1970), p. 55.

[2] Edward Gordon Craig, *On the Art of the Theatre* (1911), p. 22.

[3] Bertolt Brecht, 'Stage Design for the Epic Theatre', *Bertolt Brecht on Stage* (Catalogue for an exhibition by Inter Nationes, Bad Godesberg 1968).

[4] Ronald Bryden, 'Svoboda: a whole scene shifting', *The Observer Colour Supplement*, July 1967.

[5] From a lecture delivered by John Bury in 1965 and printed in John Russell Brown, *Effective Theatre* (1969), p. 223.

[6] Sean Kenny, *Le Théâtre dans le Monde*, Vol. 12, No. 1 (January 1963), p. 45.

[7] Sean Kenny, 'The Designer Talks' in *Plays and Players* (December 1969), p. 47.

[8] Stephen Joseph, *Theatre in the Round* (1967), p. 118.

[9] Jerzy Grotowski, *Towards a Poor Theatre* (1968), p. 76.

6

Radio, Film and Television

George Brandt

Today, more people than ever before give up more of their leisure time than ever before to watching drama. Not that the masses, in the English-speaking world at any rate, are flocking to the theatre; the stage has not succeeded in its often proclaimed aim of attracting new, particularly young and working-class, audiences. No! To most play watchers drama is not something presented on the stage; it is heard coming out of a loudspeaker or seen flickering across a rectangular screen. We may or may not regret this fact, but a fact it is likely to remain for the foreseeable future. Drama today is a form of radio, film or television.

Is this twentieth-century drama unlike the more traditional kind to which the playhouse has been consecrated for centuries? There are obviously very real differences.

The theatre deals in two-way communication, in a sharing between the providers and the consumers of drama. The audience lives in the actors' real time. To be sure, a play will use subtle compressions, and there may be imaginary time lapses, sometimes very long ones as in *The Winter's Tale*, from one scene to the next. But it is broadly true to say that a stage action running for, let us suppose, half an hour equals the same half hour of time the audience are living through. Similarly, actors and audience share real space. The acting area may symbolically denote a wood near Athens or a house in New Orleans, but in actual fact actors and audience dwell under the same roof, and their sharing the same physical space is a significant part of the theatrical experience. Everybody knows how deeply a stage performance is affected by audience responses, for better or worse.

Media drama presents a different picture. The performers are not physically present at all; they exist, strictly speaking, only in the audience's mind. The performance consists of sound waves coming out of one or more speakers, of the illusion of movement and three-dimensionality on film or TV screen. Time and space are manipulated – cut up, re-arranged and presented selectively. Chronological sequence and geographical contiguity can be played with at will. Of the media drama, perhaps that on television most tends towards an approximation of real time and space and thus has a good deal in common with the theatre. Radio and film, however, enjoy the greatest space-time freedom, a freedom recognized long ago in theory, though not always made full use of in practice.

Whereas the theatre commits the spectator to a fixed position in relation to the action, media drama has a constantly shifting point of view (or hearing). Not that the spectator in the cinema actually moves about; and if the radio listener or television watcher chooses to wander around the room, that is neither here nor there aesthetically. What does shift about is the dramatic action in relation to the audience. The spectator's substitute eyes and ears – camera lens and microphone – are constantly on the prowl, tracking, swinging, zooming, eavesdropping, retreating, leaping from place to place. What follows from this? There is no *real* experience of three-dimensionality in media drama; but subjectively it can conjure up an enormous sense of space. We know this feeling of depth in crudely physiological terms. When the first Cinerama show took its audience on a triple-screen joyride on the scenic railway, only a stout-hearted man could keep his insides from heaving. As the old cliché has it, the screen is a window onto the world.

Camera and microphone can be taken outside the studio. This means that large chunks of actuality can be incorporated into media drama. And if it *can* be done, one may feel, more or less consciously, that it *ought* to be done, since it is 'in the nature of the medium'. Many critics consider that films, especially, gain by escaping from the artificial world of the studio and getting immersed in 'real' life on location. Radio drama, it is true, still tends to be a studio product. But TV drama too has a link with reality, if only in terms of the film inserts which play such a large part in television production.

The theatre cannot help pretending: actors pretend to be people they are not; they pretend to go through fictitious actions in make-believe settings. Media drama also pretends; but the element of reality which keeps breaking in may suggest that its proper style is naturalism. According to this view, the less acting there is in front of the microphone or the camera the better.

Putting the case for naturalism so sweepingly is, of course, to overstate it. Neither the musical nor the science-fiction nor the horror film demand kitchen-sink naturalism. But it is the case that media drama – certainly film and TV, to a lesser extent radio as well – can be 'true to life' in a way beyond the resources of the theatre. The stage actor must project his voice and broaden his gestures in order to seize the attention of the proverbial man in the back of the stalls. This is bound to falsify natural behaviour in the strict sense. But the recording instruments of media drama can register the smallest vocal tremor or the twitch of a nostril.

Since its early days, the cinema has been aware of the dramatic value of faces shaped by nature and life rather than the make-up department. Much of the impact of the great Russian silent films was based on what was called 'typage' – casting non-professionals for physical expressiveness, for typicality. Thus Eisenstein carefully chose a gardener who had never acted in his life for the sinister priest in *Potemkin*. The Italian neo-realist directors liked to put real people in front of the camera. Visconti's *The Earth Trembles* carried conviction because the Sicilian fishermen in the story were actually played by Sicilian fishermen. A more recent example can be found in Lindsay Anderson's *If*: the speech-day ladies looked right because in fact they were right. The theatre, by way of contrast, has only limited use for the type-cast non-professional, who is usually ill at ease and technically inadequate on the stage.

Let us take a brief look at the mass media and see how they deal with the problems of dramatic story-telling. Each medium has its own specific conditions. One prejudice to remove from the outset is the view that, because of its technological nature, media drama inevitably makes for passive audiences. *Pace* the oracular McLuhan, the medium is by no means the message. Media drama can induce participation and critical thought as easily as bleary-eyed escapism. Well, perhaps not as easily; but is there not a great deal of non-thinking and spoon-feeding in the theatre as well?

Radio, the 'blind man's theatre', translates all action into sound. It thereby gives the highest importance to the voice of the actor – almost certainly the trained actor – and thus to dialogue. It has been said that the area of sound radio made people more word-conscious, perhaps more receptive even to poetry. That's as may be; the rapid-fire association of ideas of the Goon Show, for instance, may have indicated no more than the general rise in standards of secondary education.

The dialogue-centredness of radio drama brings it close to literature, to the theatre. Theatrical plays readily adapt to radio though aural equivalents have to be found for stage business and sight gags. In spite or because of its limitations, radio drama is at its best when it appeals to the listener's imagination. Its evocative powers lie in the play of sound perspectives, in the pitting of one actor's vocal timbre against another's, in the suggestion of a physical environment by different acoustics – reverberant for the cathedral or the public lavatory, dead for the broom closet or the space capsule. Sound effects, important in the theatre as well as in all media drama, matter particularly on the air. If in earlier days spot-effects men were key figures with their simulations in the studio of the thousand and one noises of actuality, nowadays the portability of tape recorders makes it possible to capture virtually any sound *in situ* and to integrate it into the texture of a play. And listeners demand accuracy in effects: the car engine must be of the right vintage, bird-song must be appropriate to the season.

At its peak, radio drama had become a significant art form in its own right, attracting poets like Louis MacNeice in Britain, Archibald MacLeish in the United States, Günter Eich in Germany. But since the early fifties, television has been eating into radio audiences. Evidently, listeners prefer to be viewers. Nevertheless, radio drama is not outmoded, even today, in the way silent movies were as soon as the optical sound track was introduced. It still commands millions of listeners around the world.

If radio drama lies at the aural end of the sensory spectrum, film and TV are situated at the other end. Not that they address themselves exclusively to the eyes: to describe them as purely visual media would be to go back to the silent cinema. (And even that was not truly silent, since there were pianists or whole orchestras to accompany film shows.) Film and TV drama share with the theatre the joint appeal to eye *and* ear.

Still, TV and film are visual media to the extent that eye appeal tends to take first place. While there may be long stretches of silence in a film (the safe-cracking sequence in *Rififi* is a famous example), it is not easy to imagine similar sequences of total blackness. The first quality a director in films or TV needs is an ability to think in images.

But in any given programme, the balance of visual and aural elements will vary. Even the most pictorially composed film will have sequences in which dialogue largely carries the action. Indeed, some leading film directors have made visual austerity the hallmark of their style: the Japanese Ozu and the Frenchman Bresson are cases in point. Their images are precise, elegant and dramatically meaningful but their camera work tends to be static and unspectacular, deliberately avoiding any picturesqueness. Actually, theories of film and TV as visual media notwithstanding, we all know about the vital importance of sound in media drama. Whenever sound is lost in the cinema or on the domestic screen, we have it confirmed to us that pictures do not speak for themselves. The functions of pictures and sound (especially dialogue) are of course quite separate. Images excel at conveying specific aspects of reality; but generalizations, abstract notions or complex relationships are much better put over by words.

The theatre is a place not only for artists but also for craftsmen and technicians. In media drama the technological bias is much greater. In fact, there is the constant danger that the original concept of a film or TV programme will get lost in the machinery. Hence the high degree of generalship needed to direct media drama. If radio and TV directors are broadly comparable to directors in the theatre, film direction, particularly in the case of large-scale epics, calls for quasi-military qualities in addition to artistic sensibility.

Radio and television dramas, if transmitted live, will run straight through from beginning to end like a stage performance. To that extent they can be considered actors' media. Even if they are recorded or video-taped scene by scene, they will be performed in longish continuous chunks. This is not true of film which is shot in bits and pieces in different places at different times. The shooting order of these scenes will be governed not by the narrative sequence but by technical convenience. Hence, editing has a key role in the film-making process. Long after the actor has made his contribution in front of the camera, his performance is tidied up in the cutting-room; rhythms are created and a story is liberated from a mass of material, much as a sculptor frees the imprisoned figure from his block of marble. The sound that is laid at the editing stage and which runs synchronously with the picture may well not have existed at the time of the performance; it too represents a collection of bits and pieces of material. An organizing intelligence is required to pull together all these diverse fragments.

In view of the logistical, artistic and technical complexities of the film-making process, it stands to reason that the director in the cinema is a more powerful figure than his theatrical confrère. Once the latter has shaped a production in rehearsals, he becomes redundant after the opening night (though in a long run he will be wise to freshen up the performance from time to time). The film director is at the heart of the creative process from beginning to end – either writing his own script (the ideal situation) or collaborating with the writer; then doing all the preparatory work on the production; then directing actors, extras and technicians during shooting; then guiding all the post-production work from editing to titling and the final sound mix. No wonder some directors – Hitchcock, Welles, Kurosawa and Godard, for example – have made their mark on the popular imagination even to the point of replacing the leading actors as the main box-office attraction.

While the film director – part-visionary, part-dictator – leads a host of artists and operatives with various skills, he is himself guided by the producer. The producer sets up the project in the

K

first place, finding story and stars, raising the necessary cash, ensuring distribution of the complete film. The relationship between producer and director is a great intangible, a tug-of-war of more or less dominant personalities. The production manager, on the other hand, works under the director, looking after the innumerable administrative tasks involved in film production.

A great many artistic jobs in film and television – art director, costume designer, composer, etc. – have their equivalents in the theatre, as have such technical functions as make-up and wardrobe staff. The requirements of media drama and the theatre differ in points of detail, of course; there is nevertheless a good deal of overlapping. Hence, quite a number of art directors in the cinema also work as television or stage designers. The cinema art director works in close co-operation with the director and the lighting cameraman, coordinates the visual aspects of the film and guides the costume designer. He may even advise on such matters as the choice of suitable locations and the colour balance of what natural objects are to be included in shot. He thinks in terms not so much of the human eye but of the camera lens and the characteristics of film emulsions which have their own way of registering objects.

The most conspicuous aspect of film work is that connected with the camera, of course. The lighting cameraman (or director of photography) is a leading member of the team. Outstanding cameramen like Gregg Toland or Raoul Coutard have achieved fame even with the general public; some, like Jack Cardiff, have risen to become directors. Together with the director, the lighting cameraman sets up the shots and plans the lighting, but he does not handle the camera himself. This is done by the camera operator, who works with the rest of the crew – focus puller, clapper/loader, crane operators – in what may be highly complicated manoeuvres, as when a camera tracks through two contending armies, swings out over a group of soldiers and then, with a change of focus, zooms in on two figures engaged in bloody combat.

We have seen that shooting does not proceed in narrative sequence. The continuity supervisor ensures that each shot matches preceding and following shots – that costume details do not change abruptly on a cut, that actors do not suddenly appear to be reversing the direction of their movement.

The editor and his cutters break down and join the shots (several hundred in a full-length feature) to create a smooth flow of images. The editor works both with the director, whose intentions he has to carry out, and with the laboratory, where negative development and positive printing take place and where opticals (fades, dissolves, superimpositions, freeze-frames, reverse action, etc.) are produced to order.

Overshadowed by the prestige of camera work but virtually as important is the recording of sound. The sound crew, led by the mixer, must have good technical qualifications, as stringent in their way as those needed by the camera team. Sound-recording for film presents problems very different from those of radio drama (although the use of $\frac{1}{4}$-inch audio-tape is common to both): microphones must be kept out of shot, a tricky business when the camera moves about freely; acoustic problems must be overcome in locations chosen mainly for their photogenic points; visual and sound perspective must be kept in balance.

Although a good many skills required in television are comparable to cinematic crafts – the handling of sound is a case in point – the two forms of media drama do not work in an identical fashion. The fundamental difference is that the cinema uses photographic film which has to be processed, whereas television creates an electronic image capable either of being transmitted instantly ('live') or of being recorded magnetically on video-tape. (Let us for the sake of simplicity ignore the fact that a television programme may use film inserts and may itself be telerecorded onto film.) Hence the difference in the production processes.

In a TV play, two or three electronic cameras cover a scene from several angles simultaneously. The director is in headphone communication with the cameramen while he looks out over the action on the studio floor from a gallery. He is also in contact with the floor manager, who works as his agent in the studio, signalling instructions to the actors and controlling the traffic of persons and properties. The cutting is done during the actual performance by the vision mixer, who works under the director's guidance: he selects which one of the several camera images available to him is to go on transmission.

In a live (and hence continuous) transmission this would be the only form of editing. It is, however, possible to work discontinuously, video-taping the show: this allows time for set, costume and make-up changes. The resulting tape can then be edited electronically or cut physically. Generally speaking, the editing rhythm of television tends to be slower than that of the cinema; but this point need not be taken too dogmatically.

Film and television differ greatly in their financial and administrative structures. Film is inevitably an expensive medium in comparison with the theatre. There is the hope that the enormous investment of time, effort and money will result in a long-running, profitable product – a hope not, of course, always crowned with success. Television drama, though it may be seen by millions of viewers, is a matter of instant consumption with a brief impact. The individual programme is not set up on a profit-making basis, although budgetary considerations will obviously govern a company's overall programming policy. Television programmes will therefore, as a rule, have budgets greatly inferior to those of feature films.

So much for some of the differences between stage and media drama. It is hardly necessary to add that they also have a great many points in common. The notion of conflict (valid as long as we do not oversimplify it into the conscious opposition of A, villain, versus B, goodie) informs drama of every description. So does the idea of forward movement and changing relationships. A drama of complete stasis is virtually unthinkable (although Beckett has had a good try).

Early film theorists emphasized the difference between stage and screen acting. In the infancy of the new art form, it was useful to work out its specific features. We have already noted the use of non-professional actors in (as a rule, emotionally simple) roles. The close-up, theorists claimed, had introduced a new dimension into acting which the overemphatic stage actor could not hope to master. The Hollywood cult of the star – now largely a thing of the past – seemed to support this view. Many stars chosen for 'glamorous' looks or alleged 'personalities' could not have held their own for five minutes on the stage. But since the coming of sound, the distinction between stage and screen acting has been one of nuance rather than of kind. A good many internationally famous actors – Rex

Harrison, Albert Finney, Marlon Brando, Jeanne Moreau, Simone Signoret, Anna Magnani are random examples that come to mind – have proved equally adept in acting before live audiences and in front of the camera.

Nor is the distinction between stage and screen directing an absolute one: thus, Otto Preminger, Jean Cocteau and Tony Richardson, among many others, have managed to do both successfully.

Scripts written for one medium are frequently adapted for another. Dylan Thomas's *Under Milk Wood* which began as a radio play also appeared on the stage and on the television screen; Harold Pinter's *A Slight Ache* has had a similar history. In fact, all the forms of drama continually influence and cross-fertilize one another. Without losing their own identities, they borrow each other's techniques.

The indebtedness of the newer sorts of drama to the theatre, backed by a history of over 2,500 years, is obvious enough; but the process also works in reverse. Thus Pirandello's *Six Characters in Search of an Author*, with its use of flashbacks, is arguably cinematic in structure. As long ago as in the twenties, the German director Piscator integrated film into such controversial stage productions as *Storm over Gothland* and *Schweik* – a mixed-media technique that left its mark on Brecht as well as on producers all over the world. The Czech stage spectacle Laterna Magica combines live stage acting with filmed background action. In *Sweet Bird of Youth*, Tennessee Williams turns the entire back of the stage into a giant TV screen. Endless further examples could be given of the theatre absorbing suggestions from media drama. Such marginal theatrical phenomena as light shows, happenings and mixed-media shows also high-light the blurred dividing lines between various forms of dramatic expression.

Media drama is so compelling an aspect of modern life that, not surprisingly, a great many young people want to enter this field of activity. Unfortunately, the openings are slender; there are far fewer posts available than there are would-be practitioners to fill them. In Britain there are no regular schemes of vocational training which, on the analogy of some of the well-known film schools of Eastern Europe, would virtually guarantee the successful graduate employment in his chosen sphere.

The British Broadcasting Corporation does, in fact, run several widely advertised internal training schemes. A small handful of university graduates are selected each year as General Trainees, destined for high-powered positions within the Corporation. There is a scheme for Programme Operations Assistants (Radio) – also known as P.O.A.s – and there are film traineeships for cameramen and editors. Independent television companies do not offer any comparable instruction in film or television techniques. However, there are a few director training schemes run in conjunction with certain theatres. Anybody interested in working for ITV would be well advised to consult the *Kine and Television Year Book*, which lists the addresses of all the companies.

Taking up a career in films has been just as haphazard a business as getting into broadcasting, and a good deal more riddled with nepotism. For a great many jobs in the industry, it is essential to belong to the relevant union – the National Association of Theatrical and Kine Employees, the Association of Cinematograph Television and Allied Technicians, the Electrical Trades Union, the Television and Screen Writers Guild. One may come up against the curious dilemma of not being eligible for union membership without first being employed in the industry, employment in turn not being available to anyone without a union card.

In the past, workers in the film industry used to acquire their skills the hard way – on the job. The film equivalent to the tale of the boy from the log cabin who became a millionaire is that of the director who started life as a tea-boy. This empirical approach was buttressed by a strong prejudice against any formal training, such training being 'arty'. But the international success of school-trained directors like Polanski, a product of the Polish State Film Academy, and of Jancsó, an alumnus of the Hungarian Academy of Dramatic and Film Art – to name but two distinguished pupils of film schools – has helped to shake the old-fashioned view. A British National Film School has been founded which in future years should make its impact on film production in this country.

A good many film courses are already available to the would-be student. These run the full gamut from week-end and vacation courses aimed essentially at the amateur to intensive short-term or even full three-year courses for the vocationally minded. They are offered by a wide variety of institutions: one or two film schools properly speaking, universities, colleges of art and polytechnics. Television is frequently linked with film as a subject of study. Some courses combine film and television studies with other subjects, and different institutions lay special emphasis on particular aspects: photography, film history and appreciation, film and TV graphics, animation, etc. Works produced at these schools can often be seen at festivals, especially short-film festivals; some have been shown on television and at the National Film Theatre in London; some are getting limited commercial distribution in 16 mm.

7

Theatre and Society

Clive Barker

The Field of Study

The theatre is a social institution. Through its activities people meet and interact. This happens on two different levels. In the first instance, a group of people meet to discuss, rehearse and produce a play. The theatre, in this instance, is a closed institution. Only those people who are concerned with the working of the theatre are allowed to participate – the director, the actors, the carpenters, the cleaners, the financial backers. In a repertory theatre the theatrical community is likely to consist of between fifty and one hundred people.

In the second instance, the theatre is an open institution. Although some admission fee may be charged, anyone is at liberty to enter a theatre and participate as a member of the audience in the performance of a play. In theory, the community the theatre serves, in this second instance, is as wide as society itself. In practice, however, this is not seen to be the case.

Social institutions of every kind have rules of membership and hierarchies of responsibility and reward. Every social institution has some form of organization which serves to help it realize its aims, carry out its functions, protect its standards and ensure its future continuance. The theatre is no exception. Some of these rules are very clear when we look at the theatre as a closed institution of theatre workers assembled to mount a production. Membership is open to a small number of qualified persons. The area in which each person is expected to contribute to the work is defined. The rewards, tangible and intangible, are relative.

Many of these rules are embodied in contracts which are legally binding. The theatre company enters into contracts with the owners of the theatre building to lease the premises to present plays. The actors are contracted to appear in all performances, for which they are paid an agreed sum. Hire firms are contracted to make and loan costumes and scenery. Many of these rules, however, cannot be embodied in understandings as clearly defined and restraining as legal contracts. One can commission and contract a dramatist to supply a play, but there is no way of ensuring contractually that the dramatist will take pains over his work and not rush off a slap-dash piece. The actor may carry out his contract to the letter – always be there on time, learn his lines, appear at every performance – but he may bring little energy or creative concern to what he does. He may act selfishly without regard for the other actors. The quality of the company's work depends upon his energetic engagement with the collective activity beyond the comforts and indulgences and vanity of his own personality. The company, as a whole, is dependent upon the manager and the press officer working tirelessly to promote and publicize the performance and to attract the audience. At times the understanding means refraining from certain actions. It is not the electrician's job to tell the actor how to play his part, nor the actor's place to tell the electrician how to light a scene, and the harmony of the collective is strained if either of them tries.

Thus we may say that the theatre organism functions on two frameworks – firstly, the contractual framework which handles matters like hours of work, payments, etc.; and secondly, a complex, interwoven set of personal and group relationships which depend upon an understanding of place in the community, a sense of responsibility towards its work, a respect and tolerance for colleagues and, above all, a set of shared values, which all contribute to and which sustain the work of the collective.

When a company is engaged on a purely commercial basis and the actors carry out their duties purely for financial gain or personal recognition, then the level of any shared values is low. The values of the play and production will be subjugated to the actor's or director's whims and wishes. If the production is a prestige affair, the performance might tend to be a competition; if not, it might tend to be spiritless and disjointed. This is often the picture the theatre has presented of itself: bitching, arrogant egoists and tired, dissipated hacks. Fortunately, such instances are not as frequent in life as in fiction.

More often one gets a collection of people who have very little in common in the way of philosophy or belief in a wider social purpose for the theatre, but who do have a strong pride in their work as professionals and a respect for standards in performance. Ultimately, what ensures that the actor or dramatist you engage or contract will give of his best is his personal identification with the work he produces and his knowledge that the reception an audience gives his work will materially affect his chances of working in the future:

> The Drama's laws the Drama's patrons give;
> For we who live to please, must please to live.

Curiously, the work of a theatre company proceeds smoothly when the level of shared values is as restricted as this. The level of work produced by such a company, however, will not have the cohesion and depth of integrity as that produced by an ensemble company attempting to maintain a very high level of common purpose and a philosophy of a wider social function for the theatre. At the same time, the building of such an ensemble is a difficult and arduous undertaking, to which members commit all of their working energy and a great part of their ambitions, hopes and dreams. Frictions in such a company are bound to arise almost daily as people live and work at full stretch with so much at stake.

This friction is most likely to arise from differing concepts of what the theatre's purpose is, and the means to be employed realizing it. Obviously, in a purely commercial company the theatre's purpose is clearly understood: it is to purvey entertainment for money; it is to make profit. The actor's job is also very clear: it is to carry out the instructions of the director in a way that will please the critics and the public. For this he receives a weekly wage and has no say whatever in the running of the company or its policy. Nor does he share in any profits or losses. Against this there are a growing number of actors who hold very strong views on what the function of the theatre should be. We will look at some of these conceptions shortly. For the moment, we can set against the example of the commercial company, the example of the Living Theatre which tours Europe, living as a commune and sharing experiences and whatever money is available, in which all members have a right to express their opinions and views. It is, in fact, a theatrical 'family', to use the metaphor of another social institution. The Living Theatre consider themselves to have a very strong revolutionary function to play in society.[1] 'Society must change' is a slogan which occurs over and over again in their work. With such a radical purpose, which is extremely difficult to define in action, friction must arise frequently as each strives to contribute what he is able to the direction of the company. Enormous tolerance and respect is needed for people whose ideas may clash with one another's to live as closely as the Living Theatre do. To this must be added the greater the rewards that surely derive from the support, comfort and love that come from living in such an extended family.

The problems that I have outlined above as arising from the theatre community have already begun to spread into the theatre's relationships with the extended community. In a sense, the theatre cannot be considered as a separate institution. One may paint entirely for one's own satisfaction or play the piano in a lonely attic, but even the most esoteric art-for-art's-sake concept of the theatre's purpose must inevitably involve an audience of some kind to validate it.

Let us look at some of the factors which affect the relationship between the theatre, as an open institution, and the community. I have said earlier that although the community in which the theatre is working is virtually unlimited, in practice this is not so. There are many factors which restrict the range of the theatre's contacts with its potential audience. These can be purely economic: the price of a theatre ticket is very high compared with other forms of entertainment. They may be educational: the theatre, as we know it, presents plays which often rely upon the audience knowing the rules by which they are written and played. Anyone attempting to follow *Waiting for Godot* or *Endgame* while relying only on a knowledge of the rules picked up from *Coronation Street* and *Peyton Place* is very likely to be all at sea. The factors may be social: the theatre we have has to a large extent developed out of the Victorian and Edwardian theatres. Many of its customs and most of its buildings still reflect those eras. They still have surviving echoes of a time when people dressed up for the theatre, when to be seen was as important as to see. The theatre has acquired a reputation for being 'posh'. All these factors obviously interact. The high price gives the impression that the theatre is only for people with a lot of money. The theatre presents plays for the existing audience of theatre-goers, who can be expected to have a fine knowledge and experience of its rules and conventions. The theatre therefore is 'posh'. It is normally patronized by people who have been well educated, who earn good salaries and who enjoy a sense of occasion.

Just as does the closed theatrical community, the wider community regulates its activities by contracts and under-standings. There are certain agreed practices, which may or may not be legally binding, that regulate the transactions between the theatre and the community. The man buying a ticket expects to be allocated the seat marked on his ticket. He expects the performance to be of the play advertised, to begin on time and to end in good time for him to catch his last train home. Some of these agreements are protected by the law. The average theatre-goer expects to see nothing of an obscene or shocking nature on the stage, and he expects fire and safety regulations to be strictly enforced. The management, in turn, expects him to sit calmly in his seat, not be drunk, not to interrupt the performance nor climb on to the stage, and to leave quietly and quickly at the end of the performance. By both sides sticking to the accepted code of behaviour, the performance proceeds smoothly and without disturbance from the moment the audience is allowed into the theatre to the moment the doors are locked behind it. But this procedure rests upon an acceptance on both parts that the function or purpose of the theatre is to put on plays for an audience to view passively, and with little or no significance or consequence beyond this passing of time. This is not the only possible view of the theatre's social role.

Already we can see that many of the points of agreement
that condition the theatre's social role rest upon personal
convenience, financial interest and social habits which may well
suit a certain group of people and exclude others. When we
leave the fixed agreements the theatre makes with its audience
and venture into the field of 'understandings', we can see how
tenuous are the relationships that the theatre has with the
community. These 'understandings' relate, not to the form of
the work or the building it is presented in, but to the work
itself. The audience normally buys a ticket to see a 'play', and
most of our present thinking about the theatre rests upon this
assumption. No matter how loose might be the audience's idea
of what constitutes a 'play', it expects to see some work which
can, in its opinion, be called a 'play'. It does not normally
expect to see eight people sitting in a half-circle blowing their
noses on rolls of toilet paper for twenty minutes. It does not
normally expect to have abuse hurled at it from the stage,
except in fun. It does not normally expect to see sexual intercourse take place before its very eyes.

Now, each of these three things I have just mentioned have,
in fact, recently been put before an audience as part of a
performance and have caused consternation in the audience.
Some part of the audience have accepted them, others were
bored, others were highly offended. What a person will accept
as a play and, more important, as fit and suitable matter to be
shown in a public performance is a highly personal and idio-
syncratic matter of opinion. It depends on his religious, social,
educational and political background, and often on the broad-
ness of his outlook on life. It depends also on what he considers the social function and purpose of the theatre to be.
Just as when the social purpose of the theatre is accepted at a
very low level inside a theatre company, relationships between
the theatre and the community will likely be harmonious and
peaceful and the work will be well performed and innocuous,
so when the social purpose and importance of the theatre is
accepted at a very high level, a volatile theatre will precipitate
frictions.

There is no simple way of defining the social purpose of the
theatre although people continually go on trying to rely on
simplistic definitions like 'the purpose of the theatre is to

educate', 'the purpose of the theatre is to divert – to entertain' and, more recently, 'the purpose of the theatre is to disturb'. James Bridie, a playwright of the 1930s and '40s, thought one of the major functions of the theatre was to give people living in a dull, safe world the illusion that for two and a half hours they were living in a dangerous one.[2]

But these definitions, ranging from the inflammatory to the cynical, are only indications of how practitioners or members of the audience felt. Such indications might arise out of inarticulate reactions to a performance: a person uncomfortably disturbed by what he has seen might well react by trying to shrug off the experience and asserting that the theatre should stick to good, old-fashioned, escapist entertainment. The theatrical experience is a very complex one. Its effects sometimes stay with us for the rest of our lives, coming back like ghosts to haunt us. If the experience can be summed up in one phrase, or one paragraph, it was not a very profound experience.

The theatre's social role and function arise out of its relational interaction with the community. If the theatre presents work which is totally unacceptable to its audience, it will have no audience. If it continually shows only what it knows, then its audience will accept that it will never advance. However, in this instance the theatre can be said to have a very clear social function – it is giving a small section of the population what it wants in the way of illusion and entertainment. In fact, this is what has largely happened in this country for the last eighty years, in most of our established theatres. The result is a theatre which continually plays safe in its policy and a minority audience of middle-aged, middle-class, middle-browed citizens – people, in fact, who know what they like and like to see what they know. Outside of this group are 97 per cent of the population, at least, who never go to the theatre.

But we must be wary of accepting this situation as either natural or necessary. The theatre is a social institution and relies for its operation and support on a mesh of interrelationships between actor and actor, between actor and audience, between actor and manager, between manager and audience, and the nature of these relationships give the theatre at any one particular historical time its special character. The theatre of today is very different in character from the theatre of early Athens, from the Jacobean theatre of our country, from the theatre which exists in China today, because in other places and at other times the theatre has been seen to have a more important social function than it has in this country today.

The theatre reflects the social relationship of its times. It might be said with justification that the theatre is the art of social relationships. More than any other art form, it concerns itself with the ways in which people interact.

What is exciting today is that the whole range of relationships within and without the theatre is being called into question. The theatre is embarking on a path of violent and often drastic change. Artists are questioning the passive role of the audience. Ought theatre to be more than a presentation of some distant reality? Ought it not to be an event in its own right? Should the performance be an experience rather than an illusion? Ought the audience to participate? To this end many experimental companies are throwing out the concept of actors performing a play and putting in its place an interchange between actor and spectator. Often the play stops while discussion takes place. Often the spectator finds himself cast in the role of an involved participant. Some artists are questioning the relationship between actor and dramatist, maintaining that some form of group improvisation on a pre-text is more productive and creative than actors rehearsing a fixed polished text. Some artists are even questioning the viability of any form of discrimination between actor and spectator and are producing 'happenings' and 'rituals' in which all who take part are participants. Such 'events' dispense with predetermined conventions of form and time, allowing the form to develop out of the action and allowing it to take whatever length of time it needs to work itself out.

Very often one finds companies who strike at the very roots of the organized theatre world by dispensing with contracts of employment, choosing to live as a commune, in a close family relationship. They do this to demonstrate their rejection of established patterns of social relationships which they believe are competitive and alienating, and to demonstrate an alternative way of life based on the sharing of experience and property. In doing this, they attempt to make their theatre not only a mirror held up to society, but also an ideal model of what society ought to be like.

Within the 'respectable', established theatre, changes are taking place in response to pressures from outside. Playwrights, dissatisfied with the three-act drama, are using more fragmented montage techniques to communicate to an audience in daily contact with the cinema and television. Many of the mainstays of recent dramatic method are being jettisoned. In particular, the theatre is losing interest in the rational, psychological examination of characters. Playwrights who are involved in the psychology of their characters are usually more interested in trying to articulate their characters' experiences, rather than in explaining how their characters came to be that way.

Questions are being asked about the theatrical experience itself. Why do people go to the theatre at all? What happens when a spectator identifies with a character on stage? Why should this be valuable, or enjoyable? Why is the theatre so dangerous an experience? Why throughout history has the theatre attracted heavier censorship than other art forms? What really happens when a theatrical performance takes place, and where does its potency lie?

By far the most important questions that are being asked are the overall questions of the theatre's relationships with society. What should be the social purpose and function of the theatre, and how best can the theatre discharge its social responsibilities in our time? The escapist idea that the theatre should be purely the purveyor of diverting entertainment is losing favour, and new concepts are being examined. This reappraisal has, to some extent, been forced on the theatre by the community. The economic decline of the theatre has forced it to go to the community, in the form of national and local government, to appeal for subsidies and grants. In order to justify these appeals, the theatre has had to present a case to demonstrate its value to society.

The new concepts of the theatre's social role have centred on two main issues. Firstly, the purpose of the theatre. Should it consider itself an agency for social and political change? Should it consider its job to be to educate and edify? Should it be committed, in the sense of being for a particular line or form of social development, or should it stand back and be objective? Should it attempt to stir up its audience in a partisan way and try to inspire them to action, or should it keep its distance and be a critical voice in society? There are few theatres to whom the foregoing are constant and crucial concerns; most fluctuate between these concerns and a comforting dispensation of the old mixture. But few theatres are entirely free from these questions, and the sign of the times is that these questions are arising more strongly and more frequently.

The second central issue lies in the ways that the theatre should carry out its intentions if it accepts any of the programmes outlined above. Should the theatre stay in its building and present plays, or should it go out into the streets? Should it bring its audience to the performance, or should it take its performance to the audience? This is crucial where there is any consideration of enlarging or changing the composition of the audience, and also when considering the educational role of the theatre. Does the theatre want to educate schoolchildren in the ways of the theatre by bringing them to performances of plays, or should the theatre send actors or teachers into schools to activate the children into taking part in dramatic performances? Should these performances be of plays or free improvisations on themes? Is the purpose to teach the child something or to help him express himself? Do we want to see the barriers which separate the professional artist from the other members of the community broken down and a new range of community activities develop out of integration and co-operation?

Nor must we forget that this questioning of social roles and functions is not happening only in the theatre: it is part and parcel of the changing society we live in, and the theatre reflects wider social movements and concerns. In the early democracies of Greece, the theatre reflected the movement from tribe to state in its concern with civic responsibilities. In the late Renaissance, the theatre following the Humanist revolution concerned itself with redefining Man as the centre of the universe, instead of God. In the late nineteenth and early twentieth centuries, when psychology became established as a science, so that the mind was more the subject of concern than the soul and psychologists began to examine the structure of

L

personality, the theatre reflected this with a style of playwriting and acting known as psychological realism. Today, the structure of society is changing so rapidly that it is natural that society should concern itself with the institutions and techniques through which society functions, preserves and adapts itself. Sociology is a new science which has grown out of man's need to comprehend the vast and confusing changes brought about by the social upheaval accompanying the Industrial Revolution. If the theatre is the art of social relationships and sociology is the science of social relationships, we can see that the two have an affinity and that co-operation ought to be mutually beneficial.

Surprisingly, there has been little co-operation, and what there has been is, on the theatre's part, highly speculative and, on the sociologist's part, cramped and unimaginative. Many people of the theatre resist any attempt to test the workings of the theatre by any objective criteria. There is a mystique about the theatre. The actor is an intuitive creative artist and the workings of his imagination cannot be tested scientifically. Among most of the younger actors and companies seeking a more relevant and committed relationship with the community, the commitment is usually more emotional than objective, and too often the relationship is defined in advance by the actors with little objective reference to the community.

On the other hand, sociology has taken practically no account of the theatre as a changing social institution and has tried to restrict its contacts to those aspects of the known and established forms of theatre which can be measured factually. Sociologists have avoided making, or entertaining, any value judgments about the phenomena being examined.

In these circumstances, it is not surprising that people in the theatre put out manifestoes claiming a wide, and often wild, range of social benefits that arise out of theatre, without bringing any concrete evidence whatsoever to support their claims, and that sociologists have done their most valuable work in that field which lends itself best to the counting of heads – audience survey. A number of very valuable audience surveys have been compiled which have given us information on the type of people who go to the theatre, the reasons they give for going there, and the range of their tastes and expectations. This may lead to other more profound studies. We now know nearly all we want to know about the theatre audience that can be gathered by these methods, and we can hope that sociologists, now that they have become involved in the theatre, will seek further satisfaction by attempting more searching and imaginative investigations of the theatrical experience.

There remains, on either side, a truly enormous and challenging amount of work that can and needs to be done to build bridges across the gap that separates theatre and sociology. Very little work of any depth or value has been done on the social function of the theatre and its workings as a social institution in the areas I have outlined above. Analysis of the content of theatrical presentations and the theatre's relation to the social structure is almost untouched. Because theatre has, in the past, been considered either as great dramatic literature or ephemeral contemporary entertainment, very little attention has been paid to plays as social phenomena and the social values implicit in them as sociological evidence. The study of the drama has only just escaped from the field of literary studies, and so it is not surprising that sociological studies of the theatre have been concerned with dramatic literature and not the play in performance. The proper study of this field, and the others outlined, is not rightly the province of either theatre people or sociologists, but calls for specialists qualified in both fields, and this shows the importance of university combined study courses in drama and sociology. The value of these studies is greatly enhanced if the sociology studies includes an optional course in social psychology. It is particularly in this area of social studies that work has been done which relates directly to the theatre.

Work in Progress

Social psychology has borrowed the terminology of the theatre in order to define some aspects of human behaviour which are examined under the concept of 'role-playing'. A sociologist – Madeline Kerr – has defined the concept in this way:

> I am using the term role to mean that facet of the personality which is in focus at the time under discussion. The

individual plays each role just as an actor plays a part on the stage. In doing so he expresses a facet of his personality relevant to the situation in which he is acting. The roles he will produce will be primarily decided by the pattern of the culture in which he lives, but each person will bring his own unique contribution to the culturally stereotyped part he is playing. From this it can be seen that role is not entirely concerned with motor behaviour. In the sense that I am using the term, the man's ideas, his feelings, and projections of himself as the man playing the role are also included. The total personality could be said to consist of configurations of roles.[3]

The concept is widely used by social psychologists and sociologists, and certain forms of mental and emotional disturbance are defined in terms of 'role-deprivation', 'role-impairment' and 'role-uncertainty'. Role-playing exercises, which are like sociological rehearsals, are set up to examine the possibilities open to a man in a given social situation.

Erving Goffman, an American sociologist, has gone further than anyone in his use of the theatre as a research model through which to study social behaviour, principally in his book *The Presentation of Self in Everyday Life*. He says:

The issues dealt with by stage-craft and stage management are sometimes trivial but they are quite general; they seem to occur everywhere in social life, providing a clear-cut dimension for formal sociological analysis.[4]

Goffman asserts that each man, in everyday social intercourse, presents himself and his activities to others, attempts to guide and control the impressions they form of him and employs techniques in order to sustain his performance, in the manner of an actor presenting a character to an audience.

Social psychologists are producing a considerable body of work which is of immediate importance to the actor. Obviously, some actors and directors are aware of this material, and read and study it. As yet, though, it seems hardly to have touched the general theory and practice of acting. The great strides in psychological knowledge at the turn of the century caused a total revaluation of the craft of acting and drew from Stanislavsky his 'method' – the first attempt at a complete acting system, understood in terms of man's psychology. Perhaps it is too soon for a further revaluation to be made, for a new, revised 'method' based upon our developing understanding of man's social behaviour. Social psychology deals with all aspects of man's behaviour in society: his needs and expectations, his motivations and rationalizations, the strategies and techniques he uses to pursue his ends, his interaction with other men, his involvement in the institutions and groupings of society. It therefore has a great deal to offer the actor, whose work is the imaginative recreating of action. The theatre needs social psychology. This is particularly true in the field of educational drama.

In the last twenty years, there has been a revolutionary change in the educational concept of drama. A strong movement is taking schools away from drama being thought of as the end-of-term play. Drama sessions are now part of the normal weekly curriculum in many schools, and these sessions are designed to develop the child's personality and enable him to express himself more articulately and easily. Dr Richard Skemp, in a companion book to this one,[5] has said that 'the imaginative play of children is [an] activity of much greater developmental importance than most adults realise'. Jean Piaget, the Swiss psychologist whose work is the basis for most educational drama, has pointed out that, through developing play, children learn the importance of rules for co-operation to the benefit of all. Since theatre is concerned primarily with social interaction, the rules that the child learns from dramatic activity are the most important of all – the rules of responsible civilized social behaviour. At present, too much of this work is haphazard and relies heavily upon the intuitive perception of the individual teacher, but we will see an increasing body of work done in this field in the future which will bring in the trained theatre professional more and more.

It is also certain that the scope of this work will be enlarged and extended into the field of adult education.[6] The contemporary concept of education as the process by which the human being prepares himself for the next stage of his living would seem to open great opportunities for the educational use of the theatre techniques which the actor uses to prepare himself for

L*

the next theatrical role that he must undertake. The means by which an actor explores imaginatively a new situation, then tests his experience against the objective conditions laid down by the text and so is able to build and control a pattern of behaviour within a given situation gives a framework for anticipating, controlling and exploiting the changing situations that comfort us as we grow older.

Joan Littlewood has concerned herself in recent years with planning new institutions, called 'Fun Palaces',[7] which will create the structures and opportunities in which such activities could take place. She maintains that there is much in the theatrical activity which is necessary in our time to counteract the domination of received cultural forms like the mass media, and which will help the individual to assert his individuality, articulate his cultural needs and set about reforming the institutions which will satisfy those needs.

Other theatre people who have rejected the proscenium arch theatre are looking for other social roles for theatre. Inter-action,[8] directed by Ed Berman, is representative of work being done in this field. Inter-action maintains a professional experimental theatre company which works environmentally, that is, it tries to adapt its work to the environment it is called upon to play in and to adapt the environment to involve the spectator in the action and allow the sort of contact between actor and audience that the play requires. Productions are mounted in the cellar of a restaurant at lunch-time, and the company also tours. A second group, Dogg's Troup, plays only with children. Performances are presented for children, and projects are mounted in which the children participate. In *Moonmen*, the actors arrive in space-monster costumes, and a confrontation with the children takes place. Most of these projects take place in streets, playgrounds and on bomb-sites. Inter-action actors also lead group improvisation and integration sessions in such places as remand homes, multi-racial community centres and psychotherapy wards of hospitals; they seek to make the skills and techniques of the actor available to social and mental institutions.

Although the social sciences have borrowed so much of the terminology of the theatre and have constantly used the metaphor of theatrical performance as a framework in which to examine human behaviour, they have as yet shown a great reluctance to take the theatre seriously. The convenience of the theatre as a model is accepted. Talcott Parsons and Edward Shils, in their book *Toward a General Theory of Action*, continually refer to the human being as 'the actor'. The verb 'to act', meaning both to perform and to do, suggests the primacy of action in the craft, as against the portrayal of illusion. Goffman points out the importance of the actor's techniques when he concludes:

A character staged in the theatre is not in some ways real, nor does it have the same kind of real consequence as does the thoroughly contrived character performed by a confidence man; but the *successful* staging of either of these types of false figures involves use of *real* techniques – the same techniques by which everyday persons sustain their real social situations. Those who conduct face to face interaction on a theatre's stage must meet the key requirement of real situations; they must expressively sustain a definition of the situation; but this they do in circumstances that have facilitated their developing an apt terminology for the interactional tasks that all of us share.[9]

If this is true, then we can consider the actor, not as a bohemian outcast performing three-act plays in an Edwardian, gilt-embossed theatre, but as the most highly skilled and imaginative practitioner of the universal activity of 'acting'. In this event it must be held that, by virtue of his technical skill and experience, he will possess an understanding and facility for role-playing and other social and behavioural activities way beyond the understanding of the social scientists who study them. They can interpret; he can do. Theatre in this respect would seem to have a great deal to offer social science *if* the theatre is prepared to accept the new social roles that are opening up and *if* the sociologists are prepared to use the theatre to its full capacity as a research model for the study of human social behaviour. Work is being done on both sides of the gap. What is urgently needed is people trained in both disciplines who can build the bridges across.

Notes

[1]   A clear statement of the aims and way of life of the Living Theatre is in *The Drama Review*, T43 (1969), p. 45.
[2]   James Bridie, *The British Drama* ('*The British Way*', No. 12, 1945), p. 7.
[3]   Madeline Kerr, *The People of Ship Street* (1958), pp. 6–11. This study of a Liverpool street is a valuable and clear example of the concept of role-playing being exploited in sociological analysis.
[4]   Erving Goffman, *The Presentation of Self in Everyday Life* (1959), p. 15.
[5]   Richard R. Skemp, 'Developmental Psychology', in John Cohen, ed., *Psychology: An Outline for the Intending Student* (1968), pp. 98–101.
[6]   See Brian Groombridge, *Theatre and Community*, a report on the 1967 UNESCO seminar at Nottingham; available in duplicated copies from the National Institute for Adult Education, 35 Queen Anne St., London W.1.
[7]   See Joan Littlewood, 'A Laboratory of Fun', *New Scientist* (14 May 1964), pp. 432–3, and B. N. Lewis, 'Fun Palace: Counter-blast to Boredom', *New Society* (15 April 1965), pp. 8–10.
[8]   Information on Inter-action and its policy can be obtained from Inter-action, 156 Malden Road, London N.W.5.
[9]   Goffman, *op. cit.*, pp. 254–5.

8

Drama and Theatre in Education

Gordon Vallins

This chapter is concerned with dramatic activities in which children and young people come into contact with drama teachers, children's theatre, repertory theatres, workshop sessions, documentary theatre, drama in schools, and with the practice of a group enterprise to which I shall refer as Theatre in Education. All these aspects of theatre must be seen within the more general context of children's lives and the manner in which they are taught within our society. And if we are to relate drama methods and theatre to education, we must attempt to define those aspects of education – of which there are many – to which this subject can contribute.

It is doubtful if any single author has ever adequatety defined all the aims of education. However, for the purposes of this chapter, the most apt definition is:

> The general purpose of education is to foster the growth of what is individual in each human being, at the same time harmonizing the individuality thus educed with the organic unity of the social group to which the individual belongs.[1]

Here we can see an immediate relationship between education and drama, in that drama encourages the development of individual personal resources. These resources are those of sensory perception, intellect, imagination, powers of concentration, physical and verbal skills and emotional control. Only in theatre are all these resources brought into play and exercised in conjunction with one another.

Theatre is also a social activity and it demands from its participants a group sensitivity and group awareness which eads towards integration into the wider society. By participating in dramatic activity we not only realize our own individuality and express our own thoughts, ideas, feelings, needs and demands, but we are also brought into immediate contact with others, who also are expressing these aspects of self. We are forced to take these 'others' into account, and in so doing we acquire a sense of personal and social integrity – and, hopefully, achieve a balance between the two. Thus, having exercised our personal resources and having been brought to an awareness of their nature and their potential, we are in a better position to lead a full life and at the same time contribute to society. But this is not to say that we have to conform to the attitudes and values of society *in toto*; we may, through the use of our personal resources, attempt to change society.

Leading us to a clearer understanding of ourselves and the workings of society is only one of the many functions of education. It also imparts practical skills necessary for earning a living and prepares us to become mature and responsible members of society, at the same time developing character and intellect. Dramatic activity has something to contribute to these last two functions: it can assist in the development of maturity, responsibility, character and intellect. Above all, I believe, it conforms to Herbert Read's ideal, in fostering the growth of individuality and in harmonizing that individuality with the 'organic unity' of society.

Basic Learning Processes

Education is an integral aspect of the general process of maturation. Growth itself does, of course, generally enable the child to cope with complex experiences and situations, but both the range of situations which he can understand and handle, and the way in which he understands and handles them, is affected by external influences: his parents, his peers, his teachers and so on. Inevitably, therefore, the lives lived by most children are highly complex, and to understand all that is involved in their development, it is necessary to look at the basic learning processes in a simplified form. For the purpose of analysing the situation, it is useful to distinguish three such basic processes: the child is exposed to a manifold of experience; it learns to evaluate these experiences and their implications; and it communicates its experiences, and its evaluation of them, to others.

In principle all that surrounds us is raw material for 'experience'. In practice, the situation is not quite so simple. We only respond to a relatively limited number of all the stimuli which impinge upon us: we learn to ignore the sound of road drills outside our window; we do not notice the cracks in the wall. We come to expect that people will behave in certain ways: we take it for granted that they will return our greeting – and only pay attention when, surprisingly, they ignore it. The very process of growing up leads us to expect certain experiences, and in so doing we limit, in a sense, the range of experience to which we remain open and receptive: the child raised in the country comes to notice flowers and the tracks left by animals, while the child raised in the town would simply fail to see these tracks. In effect, the experiences to which we are exposed in the normal course of maturation lead us both to expect certain things and to ignore others. And, as we shall see, this links up with one of the important functions of drama in education. Through drama we can enhance the range of experience: on the one hand, drama, by high-lighting certain facets of everyday life, may make us more aware of features that we take for granted so much that we no longer notice them; on the other hand, drama can introduce us to a range of experience that lies outside our normal lives and can thus make us more sensitive to these wider experiences.

However, we do not merely experience life passively; we respond to it, and the nature of our response depends on how we evaluate the various experiences to which we are exposed. This may seem obvious, but there is a complication. All evaluation is based on criteria: we like strawberries because we enjoy their taste; we detest the villain because he abuses the innocent heroine. There are a whole host of things and actions which we think good or bad. At first sight it may seem that such evaluations are purely a matter of personal opinion. They aren't! Even taste is subject to the influence of others:

what we think good or bad is affected by the opinions of our friends, parents and people we admire. The criteria by which we evaluate our experiences is rigorously affected by the criteria of society as a whole. The function of drama here is rather a complex one. Simply seeing a play may expose us to ideas and opinions other than those we normally encounter. Moreover, our own opinions may change as a result of playing a role, by seeing life from the standpoint of some quite different person in a quite different situation. We may gain insight into a different way of evaluating experience, which in turn may lead us to a deeper understanding of other people and the way in which they form their own opinions and ideas.

Man is essentially gregarious, and so the maturing child not only likes being with other people, he needs to be with them – and he interacts with them, he communicates. Communication has two main components: there is the communication of information, of facts; and there is the communication of feeling, including attitudes and values. We communicate both our experience and our evaluation of that experience. Here again the function of drama is two-fold. It can be a very effective medium for communicating information, whether this is information about facts or ideas; it can for instance make history come alive. In addition, it can communicate feeling, both to an audience, through the medium of the players, and to the players themselves, through identification with their roles. An historical play, for example, conveys to an audience, not merely what people did, but also what they felt. To the player, his involvement with the role and with the particular historical situation can give him insight into the feelings and motivations of the characters of the past. In essence, communication through drama adds to the passing on of factual information, the dimensions of feelings and motives associated with the facts.

All this is, of course, a simplified outline of the basic learning processes and the ways in which drama contributes to education. At the very least, drama can open up experience, broaden the criteria of evaluation and certainly increase the depth and levels of communication.

Individual, Social and Cultural Functions of Drama

The individual needs opportunity to explore the potential of his own personal resources and to be acutely aware of the expressive resources at his command, which include:

(a) The use of the body in movement and dance and in the manipulation of environment, including machines.
(b) The articulation of sound through the use of voice in speech and song and through the use of instruments – both primitive and sophisticated – in the creation of rhythm and melody.
(c) The use of visual symbols in painting, and the arrangement of objects into meaningful patterns as in sculpture, collage.
(d) The use of the written word.

Each expressive resource demands the use of concentration, intelligence, imagination and sensitivity, and dramatic activity sets up and controls the learning situation in which these personal resources are exercised. It is one of the very few areas of education where these resources are vitally integrated in the work. Each individual needs practice in moving and speaking in a wide variety of situations in order to gain confidence in himself, and dramatic activity can provide this practice. It is through the growth of self-confidence that an individual gains an awareness of the full potential of his resources. At the same time, however, he needs to realize his position in relation to other people as individuals and to society as a whole. In our present society, we live cluttered, pressurized lives, an unstylized existence, but human beings respond to order, design and reason. Whether we are participating in, contemplating or observing drama, it has the capacity to give us stylish, highly concentrated, 'focused' moments of living.

Drama is, of course, practised in the company of others and so is an essentially social activity, where the individual is asked to bring his own particular skills to enhance the work of the group. The social function operates simultaneously at two levels:

(a) Practical: the individual discovering, through practice, his working relationship with the other individuals in the group, thus encouraging group awareness and group sensitivity.

(b) Imaginative: the individual working (with the group) on problems where he is required to imaginatively place himself in the position of other individuals.

At the first level, if the work is to progress positively, the individual has to find a balance between enthusiasm for his own contribution and respect for the contributions of other members of the group. Therefore, the individual must learn to discipline himself, listen to the opinions of other members of the group and, on occasion, subordinate his own feelings and ideas to those of the group. Because the creation of drama demands many different kinds of qualities and skills, it helps us to respect the qualities and skills of others. It also helps us to consider and perhaps grow to respect ideas that differ from our own. The ability to realize how the rest of the group feels, and to act accordingly, is called 'group sensitivity'.

At the second level, we are asked to exercise our complex aptitude for living our own lives and, at the same time, entering the lives of other people through imaginative transference. In other words, by placing ourselves, both imaginatively and actively, in the position of another person, a sympathetic understanding of his attitudes and values, even though they may be opposed to our own, can be more easily reached. A tolerant attitude towards others can only be achieved through understanding the emotional and physical effects that the problems of their lives have upon them. Such an understanding can arise from a genuine experience of similar problems, but it can also be achieved through the effort of identifying oneself (when assuming a role) with another person. Through this process of identification (*not imitation*), the impact of a wide variety of problems upon different people may be understood. The opportunity to be in the position of both father and son in a situation involving a difference of opinion between them encourages appreciation of both points of view.

It is possible for the group (and the individuals within it) to involve themselves through identification not only with personal problems, but also with social ones. Mastery of the social situation and confidence to carry out particular procedures is more readily achieved through practice. Thus, within this area, there can be specific training in social behaviour: for example, dealing with officials in emergencies, perhaps the fire and ambulance services, or the police; coping with social occasions such as weddings, funerals, visiting restaurants, foreign countries, handling interviews. Then there are the more complex social problems – racial discrimination, problems of the underprivileged, the confrontation between different cultures, civil strife, threats to individual and group survival and so on – which also can be experienced through dramatic reconstruction. The objective in educational drama is, in all instances, to get the individual to become more aware of his own identity, his social responsibilities and obligations, by acting out situations tailored to his particular age group, where the problems are related to his own life.

Education is also an instrument which every society uses for transmitting, and thereby preserving, its culture, its shared norms, values and beliefs. Theatre inevitably reflects the culture of the society in which it exists; it capitalizes on and contributes to that culture. Drama is a mode of interpreting all our common experience within society; it can teach us more about the ways in which people live and have lived in the past. Shakespeare, in telling the story of *Othello*, does not merely display a man's jealousy of his wife, but incidentally tells us something about the sixteenth century. Drama can illustrate the culture of different societies at different periods of time. Literature, in the form of poetry, prose and novels, also illustrates this, but drama *shows* us, and shows us three-dimensionally. Moreover, through drama, a group can create and explore a different society, with norms, values and beliefs that perhaps conflict with its own. This can help a group of participants to understand more about the way in which its own society functions.

Everyone within our society should have the opportunity to respond to, to contribute to and to benefit from drama. Not merely can drama reflect and reinforce our attitudes and values, it can also attempt to change them, to reshape the culture in which it exists: it can be used to suggest alternatives to the present systems; it can give warnings; it can explore the relationships of people subjected to the complexities of the system and thus expose its prejudices and injustices.

Perhaps most important is the fact that theatre forms a large part of our literary heritage. Through language, dance, design, song, symbol and ritual men have expressed their response to existence. Therefore, drama obviously cannot be ignored in the context of education. Much of it can, of course, be studied as 'literature' or 'social history', through the academic examination of written words in books. But Shakespeare (along with every other great dramatist) wrote his plays to be performed. It is only in performance that the experience can be complete. The actual speaking of lines, the adoption and interpretation of roles, can charge the language with meaning and give a new dimension to emotions which we sometimes regard as commonplace or ignore altogether. A performance of a great piece of theatre can, at its finest, illuminate our lives and contribute to an advance in individual social and cultural consciousness.

Drama in Education

There are two basic modes of education – formal and informal – and drama has a part to play in both. Informal education takes place incidentally – before schooling begins, outside the influence of school and when schooling has been completed. Perhaps its most important element for a very young child is play: the mother plays with the child and the child plays alone. It is within play that the roots of drama lie.

As many psychologists have pointed out, play is a vital part of the learning process. It is self-directed learning, nature's own method of education. Play plunges the young child into the exploration of things through touching, tasting, smelling, looking, listening and manipulating. Thus he learns the nature of the material world: pencils will only take a certain amount of pressure before breaking, pencils do not bend; a stick can be used as a lever, but a metal rod is more efficient; paper can be drawn on, screwed up, torn, made into a paper aeroplane, a stone cannot. Children develop their physical skills by crawling, walking, running, jumping, dancing and so on. They learn and develop the ability to understand and use language through avidly listening to stories, through talking to themselves, their parents, their toys, through inventing songs and so forth. All the time they are exploring their personal resources, gaining control, balance, coordination and concentration – all fundamentally important to individual development: 'Play is an inborn and vital part of young life. It is not an activity of idleness, but rather the child's way of thinking, proving, relaxing, working, remembering, daring, creating and absorbing.'[2]

As well as 'exploratory' play, there is what Peter Slade refers to as 'personal' and 'projected' play. In 'personal' play children begin to learn their future roles by watching and imitating their parents; this is gradually extended to include other people with whom they come into contact. When they dress up and assume other roles – mother, father, doctor, bride, king, cowboy, policeman, soldier – or when they whirr like aeroplanes and growl like tigers, the game is personalized and takes on an aspect of drama. In 'projected' play they use objects as symbols: a pebble becomes a motor car, a cardboard box becomes a garage, a stick becomes a gun. They believe, while they are playing, that the symbols are indeed the objects. The use of symbols in this way is another aspect of drama.

Later the child enters into relationships with other children and the games become more formal, for example, 'Tag', 'Hide-and-Seek', 'Stick-in-the-Mud', 'What's the Time, Mr Wolf?'. These and similar games contain the seeds of conflict, the desire to explore the unknown and to communicate. The games also contain rules which have to be obeyed if the game is not to break down – just as rules have to be obeyed in adult society. It is important to realize that the instinct to play does not disappear as children grow older. If it did, there would be no theatre or cinema, no circus clown or pop singer, no civic or religious ritual, no carnivals, football matches or fairs, no royal or military ceremonies.

Unfortunately, play is too often regarded, from an adult standpoint, as irrelevant to the real 'purpose' of life. But many nursery and infant teachers now incorporate play methods in their teaching. Go into almost any infant school and you will find Wendy Houses, dressing-up boxes, climbing frames and cardboard boxes (which can become aeroplanes, castles, ships or cars), hidey holes, sandboxes, puppet theatres and numerous other 'toys', all of which encourage a richness of play, which in turn is utilized by the teacher in arranging the play situation so that it simultaneously acts as a structured learning situation. A child who plays shows continuous evidence of creativity and vitality. The teacher's problem is in organizing the environment so that learning continues to be fun, so that the child through his play can fully investigate and satisfy his curiosity. The teacher has to know when to supply the extra stimuli needed to prevent the learning from becoming too repetitive and uncreative, to know when to place in a corner cloaks, crowns and wooden swords so that play in the Wendy House isn't always centred on domesticity.

Although drama may, in some respects, be regarded as lacking formality as an educative medium – in that it encourages the removal of classroom furniture, the introduction of properties and costumes, the purposeful use of conversation and movement, the imaginative recognition of objects as something symbolically different – it is nevertheless included in the syllabus of many schools and employs both informal and formal methods. Teachers of drama will make use of games and exercises to release energies and develop concentration, and will also employ improvisation and set texts that require control and discipline. Drama extends the basic elements that appear in children's games by placing them within a more formalized structure. In play, children can easily escape from problems – they can twist the solutions to suit themselves – but a skilful teacher may be able, through the dramatic situation, to help the child come to terms with complex, and perhaps disturbing, situations that occur in the adult world. The child can do this through drama without abandoning the security of his school environment.

The Teacher

The teacher in the junior school will generally be with his class for most of the academic year. He is, therefore, more likely to use drama as an aid to teaching other subjects, rather than teaching it as a subject in its own right. The secondary school teacher is more likely to be a specialist – perhaps teaching just drama and one other subject. Both kinds of teachers need one basic attribute, and that is a deep and compassionate respect for children. The quality of experience to which the children are submitted while at school is largely dependent on the attributes of the teacher.

The teacher needs to be aware of his own personality and to have the ability to establish relationships with children; he should have confidence in his ability to teach the subject he has chosen and in the methods he employs in teaching it. Fundamentally, the teacher is responsible for structuring the learning situation and for its organization, especially in the initial stages; he needs to provide a sympathetic atmosphere in which ideas can be freely expressed and activity can take place. He must try to recognize the creativeness of the child's achievements and have as thorough an understanding of the nature of the class as is possible. He must encourage, help and guide the children and provide for them, within the classroom, as rich an environment as possible. He must try to ensure that once projects are undertaken they reach, at least for the child, a successful conclusion.

In the drama lesson, where ideas can be self-generating, the teacher needs to possess and practise certain specific skills; he must know exactly why he asks the children to attempt certain games, exercises and improvisations. His teaching will involve:

(a) The use of controls that do not stop activity, but rather provide the means whereby the drama can be more effective – i.e. the use of sound (voice, recorded music, musical instruments, etc.); the use of routine and repetition, in order to realize potential with movement or words; the division of the working space into locations.

(b) The use, at the right moment, of additional aids such as costumes, properties and pictures of all kinds, rostra blocks, lights and so forth.

(c) The use of the environment and the objects within it so that, by artful arrangement, they can stimulate creative thinking – e.g. the introduction of things to look at, smell, touch, listen to.

(d) The use of themes for improvisation.

(e) Knowing when to lead the group, when to withdraw,

when to advocate a point of view, when to narrate.

(f) Knowing when and how to use and stimulate the dramatic elements of sound and silence, movement and stillness, light and darkness, suspense and conflict, atmosphere and climax, story-telling, song and dance, ritual and symbol.

Drama in Schools

The general characteristics of junior children (aged eight to eleven) need to be recognized in order that relevant material may be found by the teacher for use by the children. This is an age of rapid growth, both in interests and abilities. There is growth in the ability to manipulate language, in enjoyment in the use of words – especially, for example, in verbal jokes and riddles. As soon as the child can read, a new world opens to him, providing him with an almost inexhaustible supply of material. Throughout the junior school period, the child enjoys exercising his body. Boys show an interest in games involving conflict – for example, cowboys and Indians, cops and robbers. As development progresses, there is less interest in disorganized running and chasing and more concern for games involving team work and using speed and skill – for example, football. The child will also demonstrate involvement in the traditional street and playground games – for example, hopscotch. Boys especially become increasingly interested in construction kits and making models. Girls, on the other hand, continue to play at 'families' and 'school'. Other obvious growth characteristics include a development in musical ability and in the capacity to remember meaningful material such as the gist of a story.

Material for drama sessions used by teachers in junior schools often stems from 'topic work' in the form of projects undertaken in the class. These projects may have a central theme such as 'flight', 'time', 'plague' or 'Indians', or they may be centred on a place of historical interest such as a local castle. Within the scope of the project, physical geography, history, mathematics, English and, of course, drama (for example in the enactment of scenes from the castle's history) can all be employed. Here, drama, with its exercises in speech, movement and improvisation is aligned to, and an offshoot from, the main project.

Alternatively, the drama can actively start a project or, indeed, simply be 'unto itself'. When the methods employed encourage physical activity, appeal to the imagination and prompt serious thought, drama will help give rise to the purposeful use of language, which will be needed to further the action, and to purposeful movement, which will be needed as the action proceeds from one event to the next. Junior children respond to the elements of a strong story-line: the rigorous conflict within myths and legends, with their graphic explanations of creation and how things came into existence; the super-human hero who undertakes hazardous journeys and overcomes impossible obstacles. They respond, too, to foreign and primitive ritual, with its use of song, chant and rhythm. Mythical stories and legends have an instinctive and eternal appeal to children, because they take a 'god's eye view' and have basic elements of drama in terms of atmosphere and suspense. Ritual helps to satisfy the children's need for pattern and repetition, and it unites the group in a common activity. These exercises should be creations in their own right and not imitation of actors playing primitive tribesmen in a television film.

The child who enters the secondary school at eleven plus, emerges – four, five, six or seven years later – a young adult. During those years, tremendous physical and personality changes take place, and by the time he reaches his late teens, he has usually acquired a more stable outlook and assumed some responsibility for himself. His education becomes more specialized in the secondary school, and his contact with drama will generally be through a drama or English specialist. There will, of course, be exceptions to this, especially with the growing influence in schools of physical education and 'movement'. However, all teachers of this age range have to come to terms with spurts in growth and changes in characteristics.

It is naturally difficult to outline the many and varied characteristics of teenagers, but a certain general picture is useful, as these characteristics must influence attitudes and the choice of material. (Specific ages are not mentioned here, as there are great individual differences in development.) During the teenage years, a more definite claim for independence and freedom from adult control naturally emerges. Yet, because he is at school and because his parents have legal responsibility for him, the teenager often has to accept the part of a 'child' and be subject to adults, taking advice from them and adhering to their decisions. These decisions often seem to him to be quite crazy, and thus adults come in for derision and criticism, and their opinions and authority are flouted. The teenager is, more particularly, sensitive to injustice, sarcasm and lack of under-standing. His limited experience of social situations will make him feel awkward and self-conscious, and he may be sadly aware of his own limitations. It is thus understandable that he seeks the company of his peers, who will probably provide the support he needs. He may indeed be one of a gang, and many gangs create their own styles and modes of behaviour. His activities and interests are likely to fluctuate, but generally he will be reading newspapers, comics and magazines, and watching television and visiting the cinema; at this stage, hero worship and a growth in sexual curiosity will occur. As he approaches school-leaving age, he is most likely to spend time thinking and talking about what job he is going to do; and the transition from school to work is not always a smooth one.

With the teenager's growing realization that environment restricts and influences his behaviour, that generally school life is totally unrelated to 'real' life as seen on the television screen or in the illustrated weeklies – life as lived by other people in other places – he often experiences frustration. He becomes conscious of the 'pop' scene, fashion and advertising, of human misunderstanding and the barriers to communica-tion, of the existence of inequality, the separateness of self and the need for direction. Within this welter of conflict, sometimes amounting to confusion, teachers must recognize the needs of teenagers and help facilitate their reach for maturity. The choices of learning experience are crucial. Drama, if it is relevant, has much to contribute to the teenager's growing awareness of self and his place in society.

All this suggests that material chosen for drama sessions in secondary schools will generally be more social in content than that used in junior schools. After the first, and perhaps the second, year, the drama work will tend to extend its scope from dramatic enactments and explorations towards theatre and the study of texts. However, before working on a play for presentation, many teachers have found value in the use of improvisation. Improvisation is, quite simply, a play without a script. The subject-matter for the improvisation can be derived from a number of sources which have innumerable starting-points. Themes related to basic human needs are often used: survival (related to lack of food, water, shelter); the facing of loneliness, happiness and celebration; the coming to terms with loneliness; the evolvement of community responsibility. These and other themes are outlined more fully in Dorothy Heathcote's *Drama in Education* (1967).

Other themes could be associated with the work of social organizations such as Shelter, Oxfam, Amnesty International and UNESCO, or with world and domestic conflicts as reported in the daily newspapers.

An attempt to stage 'the school play' as an exercise in itself has limited value. It should be regarded as part of a wider project so that the presentation is the result of exploration and research into theme, background, character and time. Such work contributes to the understanding of the forces influencing the playwright in producing his work, the message of the play, its structure, the environment in which it is set and the reasons for the characters behaving as they do. This preparation involves testing a variety of interpretations before deciding on the style of presentation, organizing visits to environments similar to the play's setting and research into relevant documents on the author, his period and the subject-matter the author has chosen. Such exploration is of equal, if not more, importance to the final presentation. However, it is natural for people to want to share what they have created, and it is right that they should do so. An audience for a school play can be carefully chosen and should consist of people sympathetic to the participants. It need not be a highly formal occasion, but one in which the experience is shared with another class, or parents and friends, rather than with visiting strangers.

The school play does have certain advantages. It brings young people into contact with the perception, vision and imagination of a playwright who is also skilled in language and construction. It can bring alive the literary study of a text, for certain qualities of language and construction reveal themselves only in performance. Also, the production of a play brings together many different skills in set design, stage and house management, lighting, sound projection and effects, costume design, painting and construction, as well as the creative skills required in acting. Moreover, the presentation of a play can make positive contribution to the social life of the school, and indeed to the community in which the school exists. But the following factors must be considered:

(a) The readiness of the group to stage a play in public.
(b) The suitability of the play for the school community, for the intended audience and, of course, for the players themselves.
(c) The play, once started, must be staged efficiently.
(d) The play chosen must be one the group wants to do; they must understand the language, the message of the play and the playwright's chosen style of expression; the characters of the play must be within the imaginative and emotional grasp of the players.

Documentary theatre from a variety of sources does not necessarily need a single 'playwright'; rather, it needs a coordinator to organize the material and the ideas supplied by members of the participating group. Young people can be involved with the creation of a documentary from its very inception. They can discuss possible themes and subject-matter. Having decided on the theme, they can carry out research using documents, photographs, newspaper cuttings, interviews (using tape-recorders), actual observations and experiences, improvisations and stories (both factual and fictional). They can then all contribute to the translation of the material into communicable theatre. Themes chosen can be historical or contemporary.

The technique of the documentary, although ostensibly theatrical, is also 'cinematic'. By this I mean the action is constantly on the move from location to location. Indeed, pertinent film and projected still pictures, as well as captions, newspaper headlines, songs, accompanying sounds, shadow plays, occasional masks, puppets and theatrical symbols can all be used effectively in this style of theatre. Its style is similar to the expressionist and epic theatre of Germany in the 1920s and the 'Living Newspaper Theatre' in America, both of which dealt largely with political and social issues. The roots of documentary theatre are in the ballad and folksong and in the fairground booth where historical incidents and scandals were enacted.

Professional productions in recent years, such as Joan Littlewood's *Oh What a Lovely War*, Peter Brook's *U.S.* and the Victoria Theatre, Stoke-on-Trent's productions based on local history have revived interest in the documentary style of theatre. It is from such sources that many teachers and young people have derived insight into a wider variety of working methods and additional dramatic material. Obviously, the documentary style lends itself to the promotion of propaganda and the dissemination of political messages, so that although the style may be relatively free, there is a great demand for discipline and integrity in the selection of the material and the attitude in which it is interpreted and presented.

No account of drama as a school subject should fail to notice that it is still adversely criticized by some teachers. Such an attitude derives not only from the theatre's ancient associations with 'rogues and vagabonds', but also from its very nature. Drama is concerned with direct, imaginative experience, which does not fit snugly into patterns of rigid conformity. It can appear ill-disciplined, frivolous and overemotional, and it may occasionally seem to threaten the advent of anarchy. It does create noise and is often chaotic; it is time-consuming and often demands intense involvement of its participants; moreover, its subject-matter can be 'uncomfortable'.

Drama has the power to release energies, to disturb, excite anger, amuse and astound. Tension is sometimes created between theatre and society, since within theatre there is a constant threat of exposure of false values and spurious attitudes. Suspicion is aroused when too much drama is practised intuitively too much of the time, and when it is seen that many practitioners find it difficult to communicate exactly why they are involving young people in dramatic experiences. It is necessary, therefore, for teachers to know what they are doing

M

and precisely why they are doing it. They need to demonstrate constantly the ways in which drama can help young people to experience perceptively, evaluate logically and communicate imaginatively.

The Provision of Theatre for Young People

There are many organizations, both within and outside the formal educational system, which are concerned with the provision of theatre for young people. Inevitably, the experiences offered are exceedingly varied. They are highly individualistic, being influenced by the talent, interests and abilities of the leaders and the groups involved. Study would reveal a diffuse and complex pattern of activity involving children's theatre companies, both professional and amateur, county drama advisers, youth theatres, repertory theatres, arts centres, colleges of education, departments of educational studies attached to universities, and a large variety of summer school programmes offered by numerous institutions.

Professional children's theatre companies generally tour the country with programmes of plays for different age-groups. Some make the occasion a relatively formal one, with the play being performed in a fairly conventional manner. Others are much less formal, making every attempt to involve the children by encouraging them to share the experience imaginatively and practically. For example, they invite audience participation by asking the children to make comments and suggestions during the action of the play or they engage the children actively in the play. Companies visit every type of school, often performing twice a day in two different schools, five days a week. Some companies perform basically in-the-round in the school, encourage planned participation of the children in the presentation and also experiment in the use of mixed-media and follow-up work. By this I mean that as a result of the direct stimulation of the play the children, under the direction of their teacher, are encouraged to write, paint, sculpt, participate in discussion and so forth. Other children's theatre companies invite schools to a theatre to see either specially written plays or adaptations of the classics.

Since the Second World War, the professional theatre, greatly perturbed by a gradual loss of audiences largely due to the impact of cinema and television, has attempted to approach schools, which hold the audience of the future. Currently there is a wide variety of schemes through which it is hoped to introduce young people to the professional theatre and foster an interest in it.

Special performances are given of texts set for public examinations at Ordinary and Advanced Levels. These performances may be paid for or subsidized by the local education authority, and there is now a growing tendency for local authorities to subsidize performances for schools of plays other than 'set-texts'. Special performances may be held in the evenings, but generally schools attend matinees. Some theatres invite schools to attend morning sessions, which include talks and demonstrations by directors, actors and designers, and follow these with performances in the afternoon, which are, in turn, followed by a discussion and evaluation of the performance. Occasionally, members of the theatre staff visit schools to demonstrate and talk about the work of their theatre, and this is sometimes followed by an invitation to the pupils to see a performance at the theatre and afterwards to visit backstage.

Saturday morning, and occasionally Sunday morning, sessions for young people are also organized by theatres. These often include practical lectures on lighting, on designing and constructing scenery and on playwriting; practical classes may be included on acting techniques and improvisation. The sessions may also initiate discussions of current productions, practice in rehearsal procedures, poetry and jazz recitals, and practical classes in play-making.

In organizations known as 'youth theatres', young people may take part in the production of plays or specially compiled shows. They work for one or two evenings a week as well as at weekends, and are often associated with a 'Young Playgoers Club' – members receiving special price concessions and perhaps other activities. Besides youth theatres attached to specific professional repertory companies, there is a National Youth Theatre, operating chiefly in school holidays and at various centres throughout the country.

The idea of making theatre experience an integral part of

formal education originally sprang from the policy of a particular theatre to establish links with all parts of the community, including children in and out of school and all kinds of professional and industrial organizations. Of all varieties of theatre for young people in Britain, the Theatre in Education scheme is the most educationally orientated, for it aims at helping teachers to employ drama as a teaching method. Ideally, all the members of a Theatre in Education team should have experience in both the professional theatre and in teaching. The team travels to local schools – infant, junior and secondary – and organizes and performs programmes which consist of a combination of a drama lesson, a discussion and a presentation of a 'play' or 'happening' in which the children participate in the playing out of the chosen story. This 'story' may be socially relevant, having its roots in the life of the community in which the school exists, or it may perhaps illustrate a crisis in history in which the conflicts have contemporary relevance. It may introduce new and imaginative ideas, being woven around myth or fantasy. Obviously, a list of possible material would be endless. A very important point is that the visit should be followed up by further visits in which the original 'happening' can be further explored and exploited. Another essential feature of this scheme is the involvement of teachers, for the scheme cannot function really effectively without their co-operation.

The aims of such a scheme embrace all the work considered in this chapter. They may be defined as follows:

(a) To introduce young people to the theatre and to foster their enjoyment of it in school and in their leisure time.

(b) To acquaint young people with the theatre as an art form and a vital medium of communication.

(c) To encourage active and critical appreciation of the theatre and related arts.

(d) To provide opportunities for the development of imagination and self-expression through the use of theatre.

(e) To contribute to the understanding of society, its organizations and its pressures, and to help young people relate to groups and communities within society.

(f) To foster creative teamwork by providing the opportunity for young people to make theatre with professional help.

(g) To discover how theatre may contribute to the life of the school, youth club, etc.

These aims should not be seen as an attempt to encourage young people to study theatre as a specialized discipline or to adopt it as a career. Rather they represent an effort to provide an integrated structure for the heightening of personal, social, cultural and political consciousness, to use the full educational opportunities of drama and theatre. It is a method rather than a subject, a method of teaching and learning, of receiving and absorbing information, largely through experience. It is also a form of practical inquiry into relationships, into the interaction between both individuals and groups and their environment. This is why it is crucial that the members of the Theatre in Education team should be familiar with and aware of the potential, in educative terms, of theatre techniques and, even more important, be trained teachers. Ideally the team should also include a musician, a technician, a designer, a writer and specialists in speech and movement.

A Theatre in Education team should experiment in the use of drama to extend young people's interests and capacities. It should invent and implement drama-based projects as aids for teachers, considering also the materials necessary for the teacher to carry out follow-up work with the class. Workshop sessions should be made available for teachers in which the mutual exploration of dramatic material and techniques can be carried out. Experiment would be necessary to evolve the most efficient ways of using light, colour, sound, slide and film projectors, overhead projectors, materials and masks, and all other related aids, remembering that all these must either be available in the school or be portable.

Ideally, all teams working in this way should have resources readily available in the form of technical equipment, a specially designed vehicle, a highly selective library of plays, stories, newspaper articles, slides, films, tapes, etc., and facilities for making costumes, masks, scenic devices and theatrical properties. They also need a building in which they can prepare projects, rehearse, hold workshop sessions with teachers and young people. All these resources can be shared with the schools participating in the scheme.

The organization of teams' visits to schools obviously varies in detail, but the usual plan is a team to visit a school for a whole day or several half days. The team decides, in consultation with the teacher, upon a theme. Beginning in different classrooms, the members of the team take groups of children and work on ideas, exercises and improvisations related to the theme. This culminates in all the children being brought together in an improvised performance. The team, in the first instance, provides all the light and sound effects together with necessary properties, and they instruct the children in the use of these.

In some projects, undertaken with older secondary children, the members of the team may work with very little equipment. They rely solely on their skill in the organization and their presentation of a story or basic conflict-situation, without the support of lighting or sound effects. This approach helps to destroy the preconceived notion that 'theatre' is a building with a proscenium arch that demands coloured lights and fancy costumes. It shows that theatre can be relevant in the barest setting. With only a few hand-props, some old hats and a strong pertinent argument, the project can spring to life. This style of theatre can succeed in a school hall, in daylight, with the actors wearing sweaters and jeans. When a member of the team joins the young 'audience' as a stranger and encourages it to participate, the experience can be both memorable and disturbing. It is, however, vital that the members of the team know all the time exactly why they are asking the young people to participate.

A Theatre in Education team, because of its mobility, because it has time in which to plan and analyse and, above all, because it is located in one particular area and can therefore become familiar with this area, is able to design imaginative and challenging projects to take to schools. It can deal with themes relevant to the children's lives in a way in which professional adult theatre does not. It can encourage awareness of environment and concern with the historical, political and social aspects of the community. Through group participation, it is able to take the children on imaginative journeys, spark argument and conflict, and explore historical and contemporary situations based within the local community or in a quite foreign culture. The action takes place in and around the children; it is not distanced by having the actors on one side of the footlights and the audience on the other. The familiar school environment can be transformed for a while into a 'new' and different place. The team can get to know teachers and elicit sympathetic co-operation. The visit to the school need not be only a once-a-year or even a once-a-term event, for individual members of the team can return and help to extend the work stimulated by the original visit. They can encourage exploration of situations related to the original 'happening' as well as writing, painting, film-making, tape-recording and so on.

In other words, a Theatre in Education team is a 'mobile school', an animated visual aid for teachers, acting as a stimulus to creative work within the school. A mutually beneficial working partnership can develop between team members and the staff of the school. Indeed, constant dialogue and positive criticism is necessary if the scheme is to improve its methods of operation and realize its potential. The work is for the children and must be profitably integrated in the school curriculum. Essentially, Theatre in Education provides a service for the local education authority, from whom the team needs continuous, sympathetic and positive support.

In sympathy with educational trends, as well as searching for future audiences, repertory theatres in various parts of the country, in association with local education authorities, have started schemes which send a group of actor/teachers to work in schools. This practical collaboration between theatres and schools needs an awareness and an understanding on both sides of the fact that trained theatre workers have an expertise to offer which, when handled with educational knowledge, will be of benefit to the school in providing opportunities that can be educatively demanding and alive. An organization which has technical expertise and design ability is able to make workable teaching aids and to use sound, light and projected images not merely for effect but with disciplined purpose, but there is still need to initiate further professional research and thoughtful experiment.

Any Theatre in Education scheme will be in transition, because much of its work is intuitive and organic. Its potential has not yet been fully realized. Its use and impact must not be underestimated, especially if we recognize that education is not only the responsibility of qualified educationalists but of all responsible organizations – commercial, industrial, artistic. For instance, a local art gallery may contribute to such a scheme by arranging related courses in design, architecture, clothes and social history; or civic authorities, by showing the origin and reasons for civic ritual and procedure. The court house, the local trade unions, the churches and the local newspaper can all contribute to theatre work and so to a growing understanding of the community.

Study

There is no school of Theatre in Education studies. The groups practising a combination of the methods outlined in this chapter are few. The teams are made up of people who have either undergone a period of training or a drama course at a college of education, institute of education, or drama department at a university, or they are people who have worked almost entirely in theatre but have gained some teaching experience. Institutes of education and colleges of education offer opportunities for studying the practice of drama in the classroom and organize courses to help the student to understand drama in its relationship, both to themselves and to children. Many of these courses provide opportunities for students to discover their own 'personal style' and study both child drama and theatre practice.

At the time of writing, a general dissatisfaction with the state of the theatre and the state of education has given rise to a continual search for the right material and appropriate methods of approach.

Notes

[1]   Herbert Read, *Education through Art* (1943), p. 8.
[2]   Peter Slade, *Child Drama* (1954), p. 42.

Appendix

Courses for Students of Drama and Theatre

New drama schools and new departments of drama or theatre studies in colleges and universities are being established or projected from year to year. Existing courses are frequently modified in the light of new knowledge and experience. Each intending student should therefore consult the most up-to-date lists and then write for further information from any institution that interests him.

Full-time courses at the principal schools, colleges and universities are listed in:

> *Higher Education in the United Kingdom: A Handbook for Students from Overseas and their Advisors*, published 1970 and every other year, for The British Council and The Association of Commonwealth Universities.

A fuller list of 'Professional Training' for the theatre, in universities, schools, art colleges and with private tutors or coaches is available in:

> *The Stage Year Book*, published annually by Carson & Comerford Ltd., proprietors of the weekly newspaper, *The Stage and Television Today*, 19–21 Tavistock Street, London W.C.2.

This is not a complete account of the courses, but rather a list of addresses, with the names of the principal teachers working at each institution. Some schools have paid for advertisements in this volume which describe more fully the kind of work they offer. Other advertisements of this sort can be found in the current issues of two periodicals: *Drama* (the official magazine of the British Drama League, 9 Fitzroy Square, London W.1), and *Plays and Players* (the monthly review that incorporates the earlier *Theatre World* and *Encore*, published by Hansom Books, 75 Victoria Street, London S.W.1).

Courses at universities are listed in:

> *How to Apply for Admission to a University*, published annually by The Universities Central Council on Admissions, P.O. Box 28, Cheltenham, Gloucestershire.

There is an important distinction between courses in drama and theatre studies alone (though often with a subsidiary subject taken for one or two years) and those which combine this subject with another, usually in equal proportions. The 'Combined Honours' courses link drama with English, French, German, Greek or other languages and literatures, or with music (Birmingham, Glasgow, Hull and York), sociology (Birmingham and Glasgow), history of fine art (Glasgow), psychology (Glasgow) or physical education (Birmingham). The three years of a university course are all too short to take advantage of the width of study that is possible in a university drama course and to make some headway (at least) in practical work; so unless a student's interest in a second subject is truly as great as his interest in theatre, or unless he does not wish to work practically, a single honours course in drama alone is preferable, if not essential. The Universities of Birmingham, Bristol and Manchester were offering honours courses in drama in 1970; others were in the planning stage at that time.

For universities, as for drama schools, it is important to write for up-to-date information. Each university teaches drama in a different way, and one particular syllabus may be especially viable for one student and frustrating for another.

Drama courses for teachers vary from three to four years in length and include one-year courses for university graduates. They are described in the *Handbook* of each institute or school of education associated with a particular area and organized as part of the local university. A list of colleges offering drama together with the addresses of the various Institutes will be found in:

A Compendium of Teacher Training Courses in England and Wales, published at Her Majesty's Stationery Office for the Department of Education and Science.

Details of courses at technical colleges and colleges of further education in any particular area may be obtained from the local council's Education Department head office.

In choosing a course in film or television, the intending student should be especially concerned with what technical facilities are available at the various institutions. The current *International Film Guide* (Tantivy Press) provides a useful list of British institutions. More detailed information on courses offered may be obtained from the Education Department of the British Film Institute, 70 Compton Street, London W.1.

For the business and management aspects of theatre work, there are various university courses in commerce and social studies, which are listed in *How to Apply for Admission to a University*. A more specialized course is the one-year 'Course in the Administration of the Arts' at the School of Management Studies of The Polytechnic, London.

Book Lists

Suggestions for Further Reading

Theatre History

A. Clunes, *The British Theatre* (1964).
B. Gascoigne, *World Theatre* (1968).
K. Macgowan and W. Melnitz, *Living Stage* (1955).
R. Mander and J. Mitchenson, *A Picture History of the British Theatre* (1957).
A. Nagler, *A Source Book in Theatrical History* (1952).
A. Nicoll, *The Development of the Theatre*, sixth ed. (1966).
A. Nicoll, *World Drama from Aeschylus to Anouilh* (1949).
R. Southern, *The Seven Ages of the Theatre*, second ed. (1964).

Reference Books

J. F. Arnott and J. W. Robinson, *English Theatrical Literature, 1559–1900*, Society for Theatre Research (1970).
D. Cheshire, *Theatre: history, criticism and reference*, Reader's Guide Series (1967).
Phyllis Hartnoll, ed., *The Oxford Companion to the Theatre*, third ed. (1967).
J. R. Taylor, *The Penguin Dictionary of the Theatre* (1966).

Plays

W. Archer, *Play-Making: a Manual of Craftsmanship* (1912); paperback (1960).
E. Bentley, *The Life of the Drama* (1964).
T. Cole, ed., *Playwrights on Playwriting* (1960).
H. Granville-Barker, *On Dramatic Method* (1931).
K. Macgowan, *A Primer of Playwriting* (1951); paperback (1962).
J. L. Styan, *The Elements of Drama* (1960).
R. Williams, *Drama in Performance* (1954).

Acting

T. Cole and K. Chinoy, eds., *Actors on Acting* (1949).
J. Fernald, *Sense of Direction: the Director and his Actors* (1969).
R. Hayman, *Techniques of Acting* (1969).
B. Matthews, *Papers on Acting, I and II* (1915 and 1926); paperback (1958). Includes studies by Coquelin, Irving, etc.
M. Redgrave, *The Actor's Ways and Means* (1953); paperback (1966).
C. Stanislavsky, *An Actor Prepares* (tr. 1936).
———, *Building a Character* (tr. 1949).
———, *Creating a Role* (tr. 1961).

Voice Production

J. C. Turner, *Voice and Speech in the Theatre* (1950).
Audrey Bullard, *Improve Your Speech* (1960).

Movement

R. Laban, *The Mastery of Movement*, revised ed. by Lisa Ullman (1960).

Production

F. Bentham, *The Art of Stage Lighting* (1968).
H. Burris-Meyer and V. Mallory, *Sound in the Theatre* (1959).
T. Cole and K. Chinoy, *Directors on Directing*, second ed. (1963).
J. Grotowski, *Towards a Poor Theatre* (1968).
N. Marshall, *The Producer and the Play*, second ed. (1962).
J. Roose-Evans, *Directing a Play* (1968).

Design and Equipment

A. S. Gillette, *An Introduction to Scene Design* (1967).
M. Gorelik, *New Theatres for Old* (1940).
R. Haineaux, *Stage Design throughout the World since 1935* (1957).
———, *Stage Design throughout the World since 1950* (1963).
S. Joseph, *Theatre in the Round* (1967).
———, *New Theatre Forms* (1968).
J. Laver, *Costume in the Theatre* (1965).
L. Simonson, *The Stage Is Set* (1932); paperback (1960).
Theatre Planning, Association of British Theatre Technicians pamphlet (1964).

Radio, Film and Television

D. Davis, *The Grammar of TV Production* (1960).
I. Montagu, *Film World*, paperback (1964).
R. Stephenson and J. R. Debrix, *The Cinema as Art*, paperback (1965).
D. Thompson, ed., *Discrimination and Popular Culture*, paperback (1964).

Theatre and Society

W. L. Baumol and W. G. Bowen, *The Performing Arts: the economic dilemma* (1966).

R. Courtney, *Play, Drama and Thought* (1969).

E. Goffman, *The Presentation of Self in Everyday Life* (1956).

G. Lukacs, 'The Sociology of Modern Drama', tr., *The Theory of The Modern Stage*, ed. E. Bentley, paperback (1968).

J. Piaget, *Play, Dreams and Imitation in Early Childhood* (1962).

Report of the House of Commons Estimates Committee, 'Grants for the Arts' (1969).

Elizabeth Sweeting, *Theatre Administration* (1969).

Drama and Theatre in Education

A. F. Alington, *Drama and Education* (1961).

Drama, Education Survey 2, Department of Education and Science (1968).

Dorothy Heathcote, *Drama in Education* (1967).

The Provision of Theatre for Young People in Great Britain, Arts Council of Great Britain Report (1966).

P. Slade, *Child Drama* (1954).

B. Way, *Development through Drama* (1967).

General

A. Artaud, *The Theatre and its Double,* tr., paperback (1958).

B. Brecht, *Brecht on Theatre,* tr. and ed. by John Willett (1964).

P. Brook, *The Empty Space* (1968).

J. R. Brown, *Effective Theatre: a study with documentation* (1969).

G. Craig, *On the Art of the Theatre* (1911); paperback (1962).

J. Roose-Evans, *Experimental Theatre* (1970).

S. Young, *The Theatre* (1937); paperback (1954).

Index